THE
HISTORY OF
SAUDI ARABIA

ADVISORY BOARD

THE HISTORY OF SAUDI ARABIA

Wayne H. Bowen

The Greenwood Histories of the Modern Nations
Frank W. Thackeray and John E. Findling, Series Editors

Greenwood Press
Westport, Conn • London

Library of Congress Cataloging-in-Publication Data

Bowen, Wayne H., 1968–
    The history of Saudi Arabia / by Wayne H. Bowen.
        p. cm. — (The greenwood histories of the modern nations)
    Includes bibliographical references and index.
    ISBN 978–0–313–34012–3 (alk. paper)
    1.   Saudi Arabia—History.   I. Title.
    DS204.B685   2008
    953.8—dc22   2007037493

British Library Cataloguing in Publication Data is available.

Library of Congress Catalog Card Number: 2007037493
ISBN-13: 978–0–313–34012–3
ISSN: 1096–2905

First published in 2008

Greenwood Press, 88 Post Road West, Westport, CT 06881
An imprint of Greenwood Publishing Group, Inc.
www.greenwood.com

Printed in the United States of America

The paper used in this book complies with the
Permanent Paper Standard issued by the National
Information Standards Organization (Z39.48–1984).

10 9 8 7 6 5 4 3 2 1

Contents

Contents

Series Foreword

The *Greenwood Histories of the Modern Nations* series is intended to provide students and interested laypeople with up-to-date, concise, and analytical histories of many of the nations of the contemporary world. Not since the 1960s has there been a systematic attempt to publish a series of national histories, and, as editors, we believe that this series will prove to be a valuable contribution to our understanding of other countries in our increasingly interdependent world.

Over thirty years ago, at the end of the 1960s, the ColdWar was an accepted reality of global politics, the process of decolonization was still in progress, the idea of a unified Europe with a single currency was unheard of, the United States was mired in a war in Vietnam, and the economic boom of Asia was still years in the future. Richard Nixon was president of the United States, Mao Tse-tung (not yet Mao Zedong) ruled China, Leonid Brezhnev guided the Soviet Union, and Harold Wilson was prime minister of the United Kingdom. Authoritarian dictators still ruled most of Latin America, the Middle East was reeling in the wake of the Six-Day War, and Shah Reza Pahlavi was at the height of his power in Iran. Clearly, the past 30 years have been witness to a great deal of historical change, and it is to this change that this series is primarily addressed.

With the help of a distinguished advisory board, we have selected nations whose political, economic, and social affairs mark them as among the most important in the waning years of the twentieth century, and for each nation we have found an author who is recognized as a specialist in the history of that nation. These authors have worked most cooperatively with us and with Greenwood Press to produce volumes that reflect current research on their nations and that are interesting and informative to their prospective readers.

The importance of a series such as this cannot be underestimated. As a superpower whose influence is felt all over the world, the United States can claim a "special" relationship with almost every other nation. Yet many Americans know very little about the histories of the nations with which the United States relates. How did they get to be the way they are? What kind of political systems have evolved there? What kind of influence do they have in their own region? What are the dominant political, religious, and cultural forces that move their leaders? These and many other questions are answered in the volumes of this series.

The authors who have contributed to this series have written comprehensive histories of their nations, dating back to prehistoric times in some cases. Each of them, however, has devoted a significant portion of the book to events of the last thirty years, because the modern era has contributed the most to contemporary issues that have an impact on U.S. policy. Authors have made an effort to be as up-to-date as possible so that readers can benefit from the most recent scholarship and a narrative that includes very recent events.

In addition to the historical narrative, each volume in this series contains an introductory overview of the country's geography, political institutions, economic structure, and cultural attributes. This is designed to give readers a picture of the nation as it exists in the contemporary world. Each volume also contains additional chapters that add interesting and useful detail to the historical narrative. One chapter is a thorough chronology of important historical events, making it easy for readers to follow the flow of a particular nation's history. Another chapter features biographical sketches of the nation's most important figures in order to humanize some of the individuals who have contributed to the historical development of their nation. Each volume also contains a comprehensive bibliography, so that those readers whose interest has been sparked may find out more about the nation and its history. Finally, there is a carefully prepared topic and person index.

Readers of these volumes will find them fascinating to read and useful in understanding the contemporary world and the nations that comprise it. As series editors, it is our hope that this series will contribute to a heightened sense of global understanding as we embark on a new century.

Frank W. Thackeray and John E. Findling
Indiana University Southeast

Timeline of Historical Events

B.C.

31	Octavian (later Augustus Caesar) wins civil war against Antony and reasserts Roman control over Near East
26	Nabataeans join Roman assault on Sabaeans in southern Arabia
9	Beginning of reign of King Aretas IV in Nabataea

A.D.

27–44	Sporadic wars between Nabataeans and Herodian kings in Judea
40	Death of Aretas IV
67–70	Nabataeans assist Romans in repression of Jewish uprising in Palestine
106	Incorporation of Nabataean state into Roman Empire
132	Emigration of Jews from Palestine to Arabian Peninsula
225	Persians invade Eastern Arabia
244–249	Reign of Emperor Philip, only Arab Roman ruler
ca. 400	Mecca founded
542	Collapse of Marib Dam; closing stages of Sabaean kingdom
570	Birth of Muhammad
575	Persians occupy Yemen
610	Beginning of Muhammad's public ministry
614	Persians occupy northern border of Arabia, defeating Byzantines
622	Muhammad flees Mecca for Yathrib/Medina
630	Muhammad returns to Mecca
632	Death of Muhammad
638	Arab occupation of Persian capital, Ctesiphon
642	Arab Muslims complete conquest of Egypt
661	Murder of Ali, founder of the Shia sect; founding of Umayyad dynasty

669	Death of Hussein, son of Ali
711	Muslim conquest of Spain
750	Founding of Abbasid dynasty
930	Looting of Mecca by the Qarmati sect of Shias
1096	Beginning of the Crusades
1193	Saladin expels Crusaders from Jerusalem; rules Egypt, Palestine, northern Arabia
1258	Mongols pillage Baghdad; fall of the Abbasid dynasty
1260	Mamluk Turks defeat Mongols and occupy northern Arabia
1446	Precursor to Saudi dynasty rises in Dariyah
1517	Ottoman Turks defeat Mameluks and assert control over Mecca and Medina
1550s	Ottomans begin to occupy Eastern Arabia
1720	Establishment of Saudi dynasty in Dariyah
1744	Creation of Saudi alliance with Wahhabism
1790	Saudis consolidate control over Nejd
1793	Saudis complete conquest of Hasa
1802	Saudis loot Karbala, sacred Shia city in southern Iraq
1803	Saudis loot Mecca and begin to consolidate control over Hijaz
1811–1838	Campaigns of Muhammad Ali and Ottomans against Saudis in Arabia
1818	Egyptians destroy Dariyah and defeat Saudi state
1824	Saudis occupy Riyadh and begin second Saudi state
1838	Muhammad Ali occupies Riyadh
1843	Faisal ibn Turki reestablishes Saudi state in Riyadh
1847–1897	Rival Rashidi dynasty dominates central Arabia
1870s	Ottoman campaigns in Eastern Arabia

1891	Riyadh occupied by Rashidis; Saudis flee to Kuwait
1902	Abd al Aziz (Ibn Saud) retakes Riyadh and establishes third Saudi state
1906	Death of Ibn Rashid ends Rashidi threat to Saudi authority in Arabia
1908	Sharif Hussein ibn Ali named emir of the Hijaz by the Ottoman sultan; Ottomans complete rail line through Hijaz, connecting Damascus to Yemen
1912	Foundation of the fundamentalist Ikwhan military order by Saudis
1913	Saudis occupy Hasa
1914	World War I begins; Ottoman Empire allied with Germany and Austria-Hungary
1915	Anglo-Saudi Treaty recognizes Saudi control of central and eastern Arabia, but also British protectorates over Kuwait, Bahrain, Qatar, and other territories
1916	Sharif Hussein declares Arab Revolt against the Ottoman Empire and receives British support; British officer T. E. Lawrence arrives to advise Arab rebels; Saudis remain neutral
1918	Arabs seize Damascus from Ottoman troops; war ends with Ottoman defeat
1924	New Turkish republic abolishes caliphate; Sharif Hussein declares himself caliph
1925	Sharif Hussein defeated by Saudis; occupation of Hijaz
1927	United Kingdom recognizes Saudi state
1929	Repression of Ikwhan by Saudis
1931	Geological survey by American engineer Karl Twitchell; initial signs of oil
1932	Abd al Aziz (Ibn Saud) declares founding of the Kingdom of Saudi Arabia
1932–1934	War with Yemen; ended through British, French, and Italian pressure

1933	Saudi Arabia grants oil concession to Standard Oil of California; forerunner of Aramco
1939	World War II; Saudi Arabia remains neutral
1945	Saudi declaration of war against the Axis; meeting between President Franklin Roosevelt and Ibn Saud; creation of United Nations and Arab League with Saudi Arabia as founding member in both organizations
1947–1948	First Arab-Israeli War; minimal Saudi involvement
1951	United States-Saudi mutual defense pact
1953	Death of King Abd al-Aziz; ascension of King Saud
1956	Second Arab-Israeli War
1960	Foundation of the Organization of Petroleum Exporting Countries (OPEC) with Saudi Arabia as charter member
1964	Exile of King Saud; ascension of King Faisal
1967	Six-Day War; Israel occupies Jerusalem, Gaza Strip, and West Bank
1973	Yom Kippur War; Arab oil boycott, led by Saudi Arabia; Saudi recognition of, and aid to, Palestinian Liberation Organization
1975	Assassination of King Faisal; King Khalid becomes monarch
1979	Iranian revolution; terrorist organization, Movement of Muslim Revolutionaries of the Arabian Peninsula, seizes control of holy sites in Mecca; Saudi security forces launch assault and defeat insurgents; Soviet invasion of Afghanistan
1980–1988	Iran-Iraq War
1990	Iraqi occupation of Kuwait; United States-led coalition military buildup in Saudi Arabia
1991	Gulf War; defeat of Iraqi forces and liberation of Kuwait
1992	King Fahd announces Basic Law, the Consultative Council, and the Law of the Provinces

1995	King Fahd incapacitated by severe stroke; Crown Prince Abdullah takes over day-to-day management of the government
2001	September 11 attack on United States by Al Qaeda; U.S. invasion of Afghanistan
2002	Crown Prince Abdullah proposes Arab-Israeli peace, based on return to 1967 borders
2003	United States and allies invade and occupy Iraq
2005	Death of King Fahd: Crown Prince Abdullah installed as king; Saudi Arabia joins World Trade Organization and holds local elections

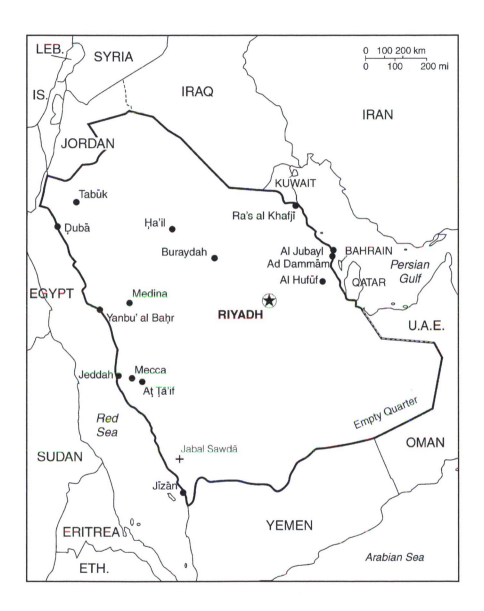

1

Introduction: Saudi Arabia Today

Modern Saudi Arabia is a nation struggling to adapt its eighteenth-century political and religious system to the demands of the new millennium. Governed by an absolute monarchy, with more authority over its people than any medieval European kingdom, the Saudi state confronts the multiple challenges of globalization with a cautiousness that has characterized its modern history. Despite the formal power held by King Abdullah, the monarch makes his decisions under the constraints of a very conservative religious infrastructure, as well as under the obligations inherent in governing a restive nation located in the birthplace of the Arab people and of the Islamic faith. A nation of regional and global significance, primarily because of its massive oil production and reserves, Saudi Arabia's attempt to adapt to the new world of mobile phones and the Internet, while maintaining its unique brand of Islamic fundamentalism, is a difficult struggle.

Unlike in most previous centuries, when events in the peninsula were of little note outside the Islamic world, Arabia in the late twentieth and twenty-first centuries is a state of critical importance. With the largest share of the world's proven petroleum reserves, a dominant role in OPEC, key political and geographic terrain in the Middle East, the international prominence that comes with controlling the holy cities of Mecca and Medina, and a major role in promoting fundamentalist Wahhabi Islam, the Kingdom of Saudi Arabia is arguably more significant and relevant to the broader world than at any time in its history, at least since the lifetime of the Prophet Muhammad during the sixth and seventh centuries.

GEOGRAPHY

Saudi Arabia makes up 80 percent of the Arabian Peninsula, and shares borders with eight countries: Jordan, Iraq, Kuwait, Bahrain, Qatar, the United Arab Emirates, Oman, and Yemen. The territory of Saudi Arabia is mostly desert, but even in its aridity there is diversity. In the southwest, along the Yemeni border, farmers receive enough rain to grow wheat and barley in good years without irrigation. This mountainous region, unique in the peninsula, provides the minimum requirements for permanent settlements: arable land, available water, and at least some protection from invasion. The rest of Arabia is dry, but there are significant differences between the high rocky deserts of the Hijaz, the low sandy desert of the south and southeast, the steppes, and the limestone mountains, all of which can be found in Saudi Arabia. Even the eastern and western coastal areas, which regularly experience high humidity of 85–100 percent, do not receive significant precipitation. Over half of Saudi Arabia is uninhabitable desert, producing ferocious wind and dust storms that can blanket even major cities for days. The largest of these deserts is the southeastern Rub Al Khali, or Empty Quarter, that makes up approximately a quarter of Saudi Arabia's territory, even stretching beyond into Yemen, Oman, and the United Arab Emirates.

Clean water is nearly as valuable to Arabs as oil, and is much rarer in Saudi Arabia than petroleum. Although some riverbeds flow seasonally, and flash floods can occur during rare storms, there are no permanent rivers, streams, lakes, or other freshwater bodies within the nation's borders, making it the largest country in the world without year-round fresh surface water. Outside some coastal areas, very little rain falls, with typical precipitation less than five inches annually. Less than 2 percent of the land is arable, and only a tiny percentage of the total soil—less than one-tenth of 1 percent—supports sustained agricultural activity. Even this tiny area is at risk for the increasing desertification of the peninsula, caused by overgrazing, perpetual drought, and excessive use of underground aquifers.

The ongoing water crisis of Saudi Arabia, exacerbated by the rising demands of new cities and a growing population, has forced the government to invest billions of dollars in massive desalinization plants, producing about one-fourth of the entire world's desalinized water. In the early 1980s, a $12 billion program built dams, desalinization plants, and reclamation systems to recycle wastewater. Saudi Arabia was so desperate for new water resources that in the late 1970s it spent over one million dollars studying the possibility of using icebergs from the Antarctic to supplement the water supply. Although these plans did not come to fruition, they show the creativity of the Saudi government in its efforts to solve this constant challenge.

The lack of surface water has created a unique environment in the peninsula. Despite their initial barren appearance, Saudi deserts are not lifeless. Hardy species of vegetation, such as salt grass, cacti, juniper, aloe, and other plants that require only sporadic precipitation, thrive in the environment. In terms of wildlife, the camel shares the desert with lizards, antelope, hyenas, jackals, several species of wild cats, and other animals that have adapted to living in the arid climate. Other nonnative animals, such as sheep, goats, and horses, share the countryside. Many sea birds populate the coastal areas, and others cluster around the oases that emerge in areas that have natural springs or aquifers near the surface.

This vast nation, at just over one-fifth the size of the United States, has 27 million inhabitants (5 million of them foreign nationals). With an annual population growth rate of over 2 percent, Saudi Arabia's young population is putting great pressure on the economy, culture, educational system, and religion. The vast projects that have restructured the landscape, bringing cities, farms, desalinization plants, and other expensive infrastructure to what is an inherently difficult terrain, have changed more than just the appearance of Saudi Arabia. The human geography of the nation does not resemble historical Arabia in very many ways. In a few decades, Saudi Arabia has changed from a migratory to a sedentary population, accommodating to the demands of the modern world.

Saudi Arabia still has a Bedouin population, but their numbers decreased geometrically during the last half of the twentieth century. While some Saudi citizens are still nomads, the ancient traditions are fading quickly. Many Saudis maintain nostalgia for the desert, and recreate the Bedouin rituals— sleeping in tents, sharing communal meals in the desert, riding camels, visiting areas with historic ties to their family legacy, and wearing traditional clothing. At the same time, few Saudis would exchange their automobiles, air conditioning, high standard of living, and university education for the short and harsh life of a typical Bedouin. Even those who have remained nomadic have adapted to the modern world, with pickup trucks replacing camels as the preferred means of transportation, and even the most isolated Bedouin tribes use generators to power refrigerators, satellite televisions, and electric lighting for their tents.

Historically, this parched terrain has been punctuated only by sporadic oases and coastal communities, but modern Saudi Arabia has become an increasingly urban nation, with skyscrapers and dense populations. The capital city of Riyadh, which for most of its history was an isolated and undeveloped town, has a population of nearly five million, while the port city of Jeddah boasts just over two million. The holy cities of Mecca and Medina each have approximately one million, although this number can more than double during the annual Islamic pilgrimage period, when millions of Muslims descend on Saudi Arabia to fulfill their religious obligations. In a region that has traditionally been nomadic, underpopulated, and poor, the late twentieth and early twenty-first centuries led to a rapid and unprecedented series of changes.

ECONOMY

Since the 1940s, the base of the Saudi economy has been petroleum. Over 90 percent of Saudi exports, 75 percent of government revenues, and 40 percent of the Gross National Product derive from this commodity and its by-products. In 2005, Saudi Arabia earned over $150 billion from oil. With the increasing dependence of world markets on oil from the Middle East, the region's largest producer has collected tremendous revenue from this commodity. However, the Saudi reliance on oil has not been an unmitigated blessing, as swings in global prices inject instability into the economy. During periods of relatively high oil prices, such as the early 1980s and since 2004, the Saudis have had significant budget and trade surpluses. During times of low oil prices, as in the late 1980s after the end of the Iran-Iraq War, the nation has experienced significant budget deficits. One other issue that relates to oil is the Saudi desire for price stability. If prices sink too low, the Saudi government begins to run deficits and has to idle production. If prices run too high, consuming nations, such as the United States, Japan, China, and the states of the European Union, begin to look for serious alternatives to petroleum. Like Goldilocks, the Saudis and other members of OPEC (Organization of the Petroleum Exporting Countries) prefer global prices to be "just right."

Saudi Arabia has the largest reserves of petroleum in the world, with most estimates above 260 billion barrels—25 percent of the global total. This crude oil is in most areas very close to the surface, and relatively cheap to extract from the sandy soil of eastern Saudi Arabia. Additionally, most Saudi crude oil is usually of very high quality. In oil industry terms, it is considered "light," which means it is less viscous and therefore easy to pump and transport, but it is also "sour," having a high sulfur content. Because of the ease of production, Saudi Arabia has a great deal of flexibility in its capacity, and can raise or lower production quickly to accommodate demand.

The unpredictability of petroleum revenues, as well as the understanding that it is a finite resource, has led Saudi Arabia to undertake serious efforts to diversify its economy into other commodities: agriculture, manufacturing, and since 2005, the beginnings of pilot programs in tourism. Saudi Arabia depends on oil revenues for nearly all of its income, but its land also has other resources: gold, silver, and the ores of industrial materials, including copper, iron, lead, bauxite, potash, and even silica, although these have yet to be exploited in a significant way. Despite its attempts to diversify, unemployment remains high—perhaps 12 percent, despite recent efforts to replace foreign workers with local Saudis. Given the public subsidies for housing, education, health care and other social benefits, there is little incentive for native Saudis to work in low-paying jobs currently held by foreigners, especially given the cultural stigma associated with this kind of employment—a reflection of the traditional Bedouin prejudice against manual labor.

Dependent on imports for the vast majority of its food supply, the Saudi government has embarked on programs to increase agricultural production, especially in livestock, poultry, and some specialty crops, such as dates, of which Saudi farmers are now exporters. Nearly eight million acres are now under cultivation, and the nation is now even an exporter of wheat. As the lead agency in this development, the Ministry of Agriculture funds experimental farms, research stations, and agronomy programs at several universities. Despite dramatic increases in production, water shortages and the persistent aridity of the soil and air will continue to be serious obstacles to agriculture, although the kingdom is attempting to solve these problems with massive investments in this industry.

Saudi Arabia has begun to integrate its economy into the international system, rather than just focusing on exporting oil and importing Western technology and labor from the developing world. In 2005, after 12 years of extensive negotiations, Saudi Arabia joined the World Trade Organization, in doing so committing to open its markets to more international investment and participation in its economy. While retaining some limits on the importation of goods—such as books, movies, music, and magazines—that might threaten Islamic morality, the Saudi government agreed to allow foreign investors to own majority stakes in the key areas of insurance, banking, and telecommunications, and will gradually lower or eliminate barriers to international trade, such as tariffs and subsidies.

RELIGION AND ETHNICITY

Islam is the official and only legal religion in Saudi Arabia. Over 90 percent of Saudis are Sunni Muslims, and nearly all of these are followers of strict Wahhabi Islam. The remaining 10 percent are Shia Muslims, concentrated in the eastern coastal region along the Persian Gulf. Shia Muslims often encounter discrimination from the government, facing limitations on the construction of mosques, conduct of their services, and traditional Shia practices, such as venerating the tomb of Mohammed. While probably the majority of the approximately 7 million foreign workers in Saudi Arabia are Sunni Muslims, with the largest numbers from Bangladesh (1 million), Pakistan (900,000) Egypt (750,000), and Palestine (250,000), large numbers come from non-Muslim nations or those with mixed populations, such as India (1.4 million), the Philippines (800,000) and Sri Lanka (300,000). Approximately 100,000 Westerners live in Saudi Arabia, the majority of whom are Americans. While they can be found in many areas of the economy, most Westerners work in the petroleum and defense industries, and live in compounds apart from the Saudi population.

According to most international observers, Saudi Arabia is one of the least free nations in the world in terms of religious liberty, both for its own population and for the millions of foreigners who are resident within its borders. Communities of Christians, Buddhists, Hindus, and other religions exist among these foreign workers, but they cannot practice their faith openly outside isolated expatriate compounds and housing areas. The Saudi government prohibits the entry of non-Muslim clergy and arbitrarily disrupts religious services conducted by foreigners. It is illegal for a citizen of Saudi Arabia to convert to another religion, with the death penalty for those who refuse to recant. The government also funds major efforts to convert foreign workers to Islam, while forbidding similar efforts by foreigners among the Saudi population. Bibles as well as Buddhist and Hindu scriptures are routinely confiscated by customs officials upon entry to the country.

The citizens of Saudi Arabia are fairly homogenous, and all are officially Arabs. Within this group of Arabic-speaking and ethnically related peninsular Arabs, however, there are cultural and tribal differences that predate the Saudi state. Over the centuries, small groups of Persians, Turks, black Africans, and other ethnicities settled in Arabia, especially in the Hijaz, but have remained concentrated in the major western cities, especially the port of Jeddah. In terms of demographics, almost 80 percent of the population is urban, just over 20 percent is rural, and approximately 2 percent is nomadic.

FOREIGN POLICY

Saudi Arabia is one of the leaders of the Islamic world, and is conscious of this role in the international community. With its oil wealth, it has since World War II pursued a course of global support for fellow Muslim nations, taking into consideration its role as defender of the holy cities of Mecca and Medina, but has also maintained close economic, political, and military ties to the West, especially the United States. With the rise of radical Islamic terrorism, however, Saudi Arabia has begun to reconsider its position. Since 9/11, Saudi Arabia has become more focused on its internal security, reducing military ties with the United States while aggressively pursuing terrorists within its own borders, especially after a series of major Al Qaeda attacks began against Western and Saudi targets in 2003.

Another key element of Saudi Arabian foreign policy is its support for Wahhabi Islam. Using its revenues from oil sales, the Saudi government subsidizes schools, research centers, publishing houses, mosques, and community centers in dozens of Muslim and non-Muslim countries, including Bosnia, Germany, the United States, Pakistan, Indonesia, and the United Kingdom. From these facilities, Saudi imams and teachers spread their version of fundamentalist Islam, in opposition to more moderate and tolerant interpretations of the faith. Saudi Arabia has long seen conservative Islam as an alternative to pan-Arabism, as represented by the secular programs of Egypt's Gamel Abdul Nasser and the Baathist parties of Syria and Iraq.

Saudi Arabia has been a consistent opponent of Zionism, opposing the establishment of the state of Israel in 1948 and supporting the other Arab states in the three main Arab-Israeli wars (1956, 1967, 1973). In response to United States and Western support for Israel, in the aftermath of the Israeli victory of 1973 Saudi Arabia led OPEC in an oil embargo. This effort quadrupled oil prices, caused massive disruption of the economies of Western Europe, Japan, and the United States, and catapulted Saudi Arabia into a more prominent leadership position in the Arab world. After gaining some concessions from the West, especially from the Europeans, OPEC ended the embargo in 1974, but oil prices remained higher—$10–$12 a barrel, compared to $2–$3 a barrel before 1973. Almost overnight, Saudi Arabia became a much richer and more influential nation. In 1974, it also signed an agreement to strengthen its relationship with the United States, including increasing security ties.

During the Cold War, Saudi Arabia was aligned with the West, especially the United States, against the Soviet Union. With its wealth, vulnerability to external aggression, opposition to atheistic communism, and personal ties to several U.S. presidents, the Saudi monarchy was a valuable ally during this global conflict. Saudi Arabia provided over $1 billion in support to the anticommunist mujahideen of Afghanistan during the Soviet Union's occupation of that country (1979–1989), and also provided aid to other anticommunist resistance movements in Africa and Latin America, although these actions had unintended consequences, including training the future leaders of international terrorism. During the Gulf War of 1991, the Saudis provided indispensable basing rights, financial and logistical support, and military forces to assist in the liberation of Kuwait. The support for Iraq by Jordan, Yemen, and the Palestinians angered the Saudis, who in response expelled millions of students and workers from these countries who were resident in the kingdom. Since the end of the Cold War, and the rise of Islamic terrorism, the Saudi government has attempted to reduce the reasons for anti-Western sentiments in the kingdom, most notably by negotiating for the withdrawal of U.S. military forces, a process largely completed by late 2003.

Saudi Arabia is a participant in many international organizations, including the United Nations, the World Bank, the International Monetary Fund, the Arab League, and the Organization of the Islamic Conference. The Saudis are the leading nation in two other groups, the Gulf Cooperation Council, an organization of conservative oil-rich monarchies in the region, and the Organization of Petroleum Exporting Countries, whose nations attempt to maintain oil prices at stable and profitable levels through assigning quotas and production goals. A major donor to developing nations, Saudi Arabia contributes 4 percent of its GDP annually to foreign aid. Amounting to approximately $17 billion per year, this places Saudi Arabia behind only the United States in absolute terms, but the most generous in the world by the percentage of national income spent on aid. The United States, by comparison, spends less than 1 percent of its GDP on foreign assistance, although private donations, if counted in, would raise this figure substantially.

NATIONAL SECURITY

Saudi Arabia is a rich nation in a dangerous region, and so the monarchy has followed the belief for many decades that preservation of this wealth depends on close ties to the United States—the only nation with the present capability of assisting in the defense of the oil fields, as well as providing the weapons and training to equip the Saudi military. Events over the past two decades, from the Gulf War to the U.S. invasion of Iraq, have placed tensions on this relationship, but not ended the tie between the United States and Saudi Arabia. Despite recent reconsiderations of the U.S.-Saudi security partnership, its continuation reflects the challenges for Saudi defense. The two most persistent security problems of Saudi Arabia remain: defending its vast territory and oil against external threats, and preserving its internal peace in an environment of rising social tensions, international terrorism, and questions about the long-term stability and viability of the government of Saudi Arabia.

The branches of the Saudi armed forces are the Royal Saudi Land Forces, Royal Saudi Naval Forces, Royal Saudi Air Force, and the Royal Saudi Air Defense Forces. Each of these all-male branches relies on volunteers to staff the 125,000-man active duty force. The Land Forces provide for the defense of the national territory against external threats, and supplied with U.S.-made M1 battle tanks, played a major role in the 1991 liberation of Kuwait. As a result of billions of dollars in acquisitions, the Saudi Air Force has significant combat capabilities, and by most estimates is second only to Israel in its overall power.

Its main strike force is a fleet of U.S. and British aircraft, including F-15 fighter-bombers. The navy and air defense forces are more modest, protecting Saudi coasts and airspace against potential aggression.

In addition to these conventional forces, Saudi Arabia has a National Guard of 75,000. This organization's missions are to safeguard the royal family, preserve internal security, defend the holy cities of Mecca and Medina, defeat coup attempts, and protect strategic facilities. Recruited from tribes loyal to the regime, its 25,000 active personnel have reserve and militia units sufficient to provide an additional 50,000 personnel. The National Guard is a direct descendant of the Ikhwan tribal order that played such a critical role in the wars for the creation of Saudi Arabia. Although it is primarily a domestic force, National Guard units had a key role in the Gulf War, fighting against Iraqi army units in Kuwait and during the battle of Khafji, when a small Iraqi army unit occupied the Saudi city.

Despite the tremendous military spending of the monarchy, the Saudi military has struggled to field an effective force. In the early 1990s, the kingdom's armed forces, faced with a hostile Iran and Iraq, made significant efforts to develop and train competent ground and air forces, spending several billion dollars on armaments and training. Since 9/11 and the U.S. invasion of Iraq, however, open United States–Saudi ties have declined significantly: the United States evacuated nearly all of its personnel from Saudi Arabia, moving its command centers and aircraft to Qatar, Bahrain, Kuwait, and Iraq. After reaching a post-Gulf War height of over 5,000 personnel in the late 1990s, by early 2004 there were approximately 500 U.S. military service members on duty. Despite the reduction in military ties, the two nations continue to collaborate in many areas, including training and intelligence, and U.S. contractors provide indispensable training, maintenance, and logistics assistance to the Saudi armed forces at all levels.

Despite the decline in a conventional threat from Iraq, Saudi Arabian security planners still see potential challenges. Iran continues to be a force for instability in the region, a worry for Saudi Arabia given its own Shia minority in eastern Saudi Arabia, as well as the close ties between Iran and some Iraqi Shia parties. The porous border with Yemen presents a potential entry for smugglers, terrorists, and illegal aliens. Relations between Yemen and Saudi Arabia reached their lowest point in 1990, when the Saudi government expelled over one million Yemenis to protest their government's support for Iraq in the Gulf War. Tensions have lessened, but remain present. Finally, the Israeli military remains the strongest in the region, and a high percentage of Saudi military forces focus on the northwestern sectors against this potential threat, should a broader Middle Eastern war against Israel involve the Saudi military.

FAMILY LIFE AND THE STATUS OF WOMEN

While it may be a truism that families are the building blocks of society, nowhere is this more accurate than in Saudi Arabia. The Saudi absolute monarchy is a reflection of the importance of ties of blood and marriage. Just as the most important positions in the government and military remain with the Saudi princes, so typical Saudi Arabian families place their greatest trust and dependence upon members of their extended family. The extended family and groups of extended families, the clans, organize themselves around the male relatives, and do everything they can to assist one another to gain advantages in society.

Loyalties diminish the farther away one gets from the family. In decreasing order of loyalty, Saudis owe their allegiance to their family, clan, tribe, and nation. Practices that in the West would be considered unacceptable—hiring relatives for government positions, excluding contractors on the basis of their tribal origins, marrying first and second cousins—are not only acceptable in Saudi Arabia, but expected ways of living and doing business. The honor of the family, clan, tribe, and nation is very important to most Saudis, and defending this honor remains one of the most important social imperatives, even to the point of murdering family members—such as girls who have had sex outside of marriage—who might shame the family name. Although these "honor killings" have decreased in recent years, they remain a serious legal and moral challenge in Saudi society.

Women in Saudi Arabia face significant restrictions on their lives, limitations that stem from Arab history as well as a fundamentalist interpretation of the Quran and other early Islamic writings. Although most Islamic countries have more conservative views of relations between the sexes than does the West, Saudi Arabia's Wahhabi version of Islam places it at the far end of this spectrum. Several of Saudi Arabia's most well-known customs in regards to women are beginning to change in modest ways, but these rules remain enforced in Saudi Arabia. Veiling is common in Arab and Muslim countries, but in Saudi Arabia this takes the form of the abaya—a full-length robe or cloak that covers the entire body—and the hijab, or head covering. The face veil is optional in some regions and tribal areas, but very common. While the face veil is optional, nonexpatriate women in Saudi Arabia must at a minimum cover their hair and neck. The Quran and Hadith direct Muslim women to dress modestly, although there is significant debate within the Islamic world about the implications of this injunction. The Prophet Mohammed's first wife, Khadijah, did not wear a veil, for example, and engaged in commercial, political, and religious activities in mixed company.

Another visible element of the status of women in Saudi Arabia is their seclusion from public view. While the old saying that a woman should leave home twice—to marry and to attend her own funeral—is perhaps an over-statement, it does have some historical truth. Women do not have the right to travel, in Saudi Arabia or overseas, without the permission of their fathers or husband, cannot legally drive, and cannot hold government positions, with a few exceptions. Women have limited professional choices in Saudi Arabia. For the most part, their vocational choices remain confined to all-female environments, including schools and medical clinics. While women can attain the same educational level as men, through attending all-female sections of universities, once they complete these degrees they often have difficulty finding employment appropriate to their training and compatible with official views of honor. While since the early 1990s there have been more opportunities for women to serve as engineers, doctors, teachers, and in other professional positions, as recently as 1990, fewer than 200,000 Saudi women worked, out of approximately 10 million women.

Under the strict form of Islamic law (sharia) practiced in Saudi Arabia, women have few legal rights. Throughout her life, a Saudi woman is subject to a man. Until she marries, her father retains absolute authority. After marriage, her husband takes this authority. In the absence of her father or husband, her brothers, uncles, and other male relatives can restrict her behavior, work, education, and other living conditions. In case of divorce, a woman must return to her father's house, or that of another male relative. Although these rules are in place ostensibly to protect women and preserve their familial honor and sexual purity, in practice they confine women to a very small world of family and friends.

Marriage in Saudi Arabia is contractual, with rights and obligations established by means of a formal prenuptial agreement. Depending on the terms of the marriage contract, and the relative strength of the two families, a woman can maintain some autonomy over her financial resources, an easier means to divorce and, as is very common, her own name. Men still retain significant strength by sharia tradition. In case of divorce, they receive custody of all children—boys at the age of seven and girls at the age of nine—and can marry as many as four wives, so long as they support each one equally financially. Although increasingly rare, polygamy continues, and it is not uncommon to see three or four identical houses in Saudi Arabia—one for each wife. A woman's testimony is worth half that of a man's in legal proceedings, and daughters inherit half the amount of their brothers from their father's bequest.

Despite these legal, cultural, and social restrictions, women do have some authority in Saudi Arabia. While men control public life, women have significant power within the home. While the husband controls the destiny of the family in the public sphere, he is not the master once he passes over the threshold. Women are heavily involved in finding suitable husbands for their daughters, and control internal family finances. Outside the home, however, they remain subordinate in all areas. These rules apply most particularly to Saudi Arabia: when traveling or studying abroad, even in other Arab countries, few Saudi women wear the face veil or remain segregated from public view.

EDUCATION

Saudi Arabia was a late arrival in the field of education. Although most of Saudi Arabia's territory remained free of foreign occupation, one disadvantage of this was the lack of schools and educational ties that British, Ottoman, or other imperial states might have provided in the eighteenth and nineteenth centuries. Even in the areas that were occupied by the Turks—especially the Hijaz—the handful of schools established serviced primarily the children of Ottoman officials. After the establishment of the Saudi state in 1902, the peninsula experienced 30 years of civil war and insurrection, delaying the possibility of a normal educational process. While the kingdom began to establish some schools in the 1930s and 1940s, it was not until 1954 that Saudi Arabia mandated elementary schooling for boys. Shortages of schools and resistance by conservatives to the inclusion of secular subjects meant that even these modest steps met resistance. In 1960, the kingdom expanded this program to include girls as well. At the first school in Buraidah, in the central province of Al Qasim, the only student during its initial year of operation was the daughter of the female principal.

Faced with this resistance, the Saudi government has taken a very cautious and deliberate approach to education, and has still not made it compulsory. The government also allows private schools, although these must meet strict guidelines to operate. To prevent opposition from the clergy, the state has enshrined religious teaching at all levels through the university. Wahhabi scholars and imams have significant input into textbooks, curriculum, examinations, and courses of study through the four levels of public education—preschool, elementary, intermediate, and secondary.

Higher education is also a relatively new phenomenon in Saudi Arabia, with the first institution, King Saud University, founded in 1957. By 2000, there were almost 90 postsecondary institutions: universities, colleges, and technical schools. To cope with the domestic demand for university education, the government during the 1960s and 1970s also spent tremendous sums of money sending students abroad to earn degrees, especially in the United States and United Kingdom. Undergraduate and graduate degrees from foreign universities are still considered more prestigious than those from Saudi institutions, and are tremendous assets to those seeking government employment or promotions.

In recent years, Saudi Arabia has educated so many students that it now has a surplus of college graduates, especially in fields such as Islamic theology, Arabic language, and sharia law, adding to tensions among the young adult population. Without prospects for employment that they believe is appropriate to their education and sense of honor, they are a potential source for social problems. The higher emphasis historically placed on the education of males explains the ongoing disparity between the literacy rate of males—85 percent—and females—78 percent—although these figures are narrower among the newer generations. By most estimates, women now comprise a majority of university students, although they have even fewer job opportunities than males in overrepresented fields.

LEGAL SYSTEM AND CIVIL RIGHTS

Saudi Arabia follows sharia (Islamic law), with the Quran as the official constitution of the country. This makes Saudi Arabia unique by its enshrining of a religious text as a political document. One of the most important reasons that the government is legitimized is its willingness to enforce sharia in the land that gave birth to Islam. In addition, the decrees issued by the king have legal force as the Basic Law, and are considered binding on all citizens. The Wahhabi interpretation of sharia takes the Quran and Hadith at their most literal levels.

One result of this embrace of sharia is that criminal penalties in Saudi Arabia are very severe. The death penalty can be, and usually is, imposed for murder and rape, and can also be the punishment for adultery and conversion to a religion other than Islam, although in practice executions for these two crimes are rare. Convicted thieves may have their hands amputated; the open use of alcohol or, especially, illegal drugs can lead to long prison sentences. Although these penalties are harsh, and often punish behavior that is legal in most countries in the world, Saudis argue that their crime rates are among the lowest in the world.

Religious scholars (the ulama) hold tremendous influence in Saudi Arabia. The king regularly meets with prominent representatives of this class, whose ability to interpret the Quran and sharia can give legitimacy to the decisions of the king, or cause the monarchy trouble by withholding this support. The most prominent scholars serve on the Supreme Judicial Council, an official advisory body created in the early 1970s to provide recommendations to the Ministry of Justice and to the king. The recent rulings of this council, whether supporting the Gulf War, condemning Al Qaeda, or endorsing limited elections, can assist the kingdom in promoting ideas that might have some opposition among the Saudi population.

The court system is complex. At the bottom are qadis, or judges, who preside over minor criminal and civil cases in local summary courts. In most cases, one qadi decides a case on its merits, following sharia, the Basic Law, and Saudi traditions. High courts are the next level, and often use a panel of three qadis to decide these cases. Above the high courts are two courts of appeal, which have the same powers, in Mecca and Riyadh. After a decision at the high court, plaintiffs and defendants can lodge a final appeal personally to the king. Saudi judges take a very active role in the court, questioning plaintiffs, defendants, and witnesses themselves, and deciding on punishment. Courts place a great deal of importance on eyewitnesses, confessions, and other testimony, both because of the importance of these kinds of evidence in Islamic tradition, and because of the limited investigative means available to most Saudi police and investigators.

POLITICAL SYSTEM

The Kingdom of Saudi Arabia, as indicated in its official title, is a monarchy. The current ruler, Abdullah bin Abdul Aziz Al Saud, is not only king but also prime minister and Custodian of the Two Holy Mosques, the latter title held to signify Abdullah's responsibility to maintain free access to Mecca and Medina during the hajj (holy pilgrimage to visit these cities). More specifically, Saudi Arabia is an absolute monarchy under the control of the Saudi royal family—the direct male descendants of King Abd Al-Aziz, more commonly known as Ibn Saud. Although they have no institutional limits on their power, in practice their authority is confined by tradition, sharia (Islamic law), and pressure groups within the vast royal family. The king appoints his own successor from the royal princes, although in practice his choice must receive the support of a clear majority of the approximately 500 potential candidates for this position, following the Basic Law, a decree issued in 1992 by then King Fahd.

Saudi Arabia does not have a modern written constitution, elected legislature, or national court system with the ability to check the king's actions, although in recent years the courts have become more active. The government claims that the only constitution that Saudi Arabia needs is the Quran, but the scripture's discussions of the structure of government do not provide sufficient guidance in this area. Religious leaders can give advice to the monarch, but his are the final decisions, even in matters of religious law. The king's powers in theory are absolute: he issues all laws and decrees, personally appoints key officials in the state, diplomatic corps, and officers above the rank of lieutenant colonel, serves as commander-in-chief, and is the court of last resort for all legal appeals unsatisfied by the judicial system.

To assist with his duties, the king has a Council of Ministers, made up of the executives of the principal branches of government. Created in 1953, this body includes approximately 25 cabinet-level officials, and coordinates the most important practical decisions of Saudi Arabia. The ministers prepare royal decrees, advise the king, and implement his decisions in the country. Taking into account the interest groups in the country, the key ministries are usually held by members of the royal family, representatives of the most important tribes, and well-educated technocrats, many with advanced degrees from foreign universities.

To handle routine government affairs and provide personal advice, the king also has a smaller body, the Royal Diwan, staffed by his closest advisors, as well as special departments in the government, such as the Office of Bedouin Affairs and the well-known Committees for the Propagation of Virtue and Prevention of Vice, the moral police who are charged with enforcing public morals, such as mandating wearing of the full veil and abaya (black overgarment) by women. The kings also practice a tradition known as the majlis (personal audience), by which common Saudi citizens can petition the monarch directly for favors, redress of grievances, or to appeal decisions of government officials. Although this practice has become less useful as the Saudi population has increased along with the complexity of problems, subjects may still present written petitions with the possibility of being granted a personal audience with the king.

A new government institution, the Consultative Council, also provides advice to the monarch and ministries, and consists of committees devoted to economic affairs, national security, Islamic affairs, and other issues. The king appoints the 150 members of the council. Although it has not yet become a strong legislative body and all members serve at the pleasure of the king, the government has announced that the Consultative Council will gain additional responsibilities over the next few years, and some officials suggest that eventually some of the positions may be elected. This body is consistent with the Arab tradition of leadership, which expects tribal chiefs and other men in prominent positions to consult elders and religious leaders to build consensus for major decisions.

At the local level, Saudi Arabia has 13 provinces, each administered by a governor chosen by the king. Although Saudi Arabia is officially highly centralized, with decisions about education, law, police affairs, religion, and other issues made in Riyadh, governors have some autonomy in applying these decisions to local conditions. The most important mission of the governors is to safeguard internal security, especially in the four key provinces—Mecca, Medina, Riyadh, and the oil-rich Eastern Province—upon which the economy and prestige rest. Key ministries in the capital work with the governors, who are usually members of the royal family, to promote development, consistency, and stability. Governors also are expected to hold majlis (personal audiences), as at the national level, where citizens can petition for assistance or to resolve disputes. There are also appointed councils in each of the provinces, although their authority remains limited.

In 2005, Saudi Arabia held its first free local elections in its history, choosing half of the members of municipal councils in Mecca, Medina, Riyadh, and almost 200 other cities and towns. While women and members of the military could not vote, the elections were generally free and fair, and several government officials indicated their hope that Saudi women would be allowed to vote in the 2009 elections. While political parties and electoral lists are illegal in Saudi Arabia, the majority of winners seem to have had the backing of a religious coalition known as the Golden List. Although dedicated to the official ideology of Wahhabi Islam, many of the leaders of this coalition were educated in the West and have indicated their desire for moderate reform. Given the modest responsibilities of these councils, this experiment is in keeping with the glacial pace of change in the kingdom.

CONCLUSION

Saudi Arabia is a rich country beset by a number of serious problems: modernizing while preserving traditions, allowing more opportunities for women without jeopardizing conservative social values, diversifying the economy of a nation poor in resources other than petroleum, managing internal and external threats to national security, and balancing economic and political ties to the West without becoming a Western nation. Saudi Arabia's policy of accepting a rapid transformation of its economy, while attempting to move very slowly toward political, social, and cultural adaptation, has exposed serious tensions within its society, as well as tensions with the international community. The success or failure of the Saudis to develop solutions to their difficulties, without causing unmanageable stress on their society, will be an extreme test of their ability not just to progress, but to survive as a state and nation in the contemporary world.

2

Arabia before Muhammad (to 570 A.D.)

BACKGROUND

From the earliest period of human occupation, the Arabian Peninsula—one-third the size of the United States—was a crossroads of ideas, empires, trade, religions, ethnic groups, and languages. Never completely ruled by any external force, the Arabs and other residents of the region were nonetheless deeply affected by developments in the ancient world. During this period in the history of Arabia, the Arabs developed a spoken and written language, the primary elements of the Bedouin culture, their style of fighting, and their importance as unruly residents of a terrain under contention between empires.

Arabia's commercial value during the ancient period did not derive merely from its central place between Africa and Asia, between the Greco-Roman worlds and the states of Asia. The Arabs also produced products that were valuable and rare: frankincense and myrrh, two forms of incense used for religious rituals and embalming, and made most famous in the Western world through their mention in the New Testament as gifts to Jesus at his birth (the gospel of Matthew, chapter 2, verse 11). Brought at great expense on the backs of camels from Oman and Yemen to the borders with the Hellenistic and later Roman Empires, these two aromatic products provided great value to the merchants who were able to transport them across Arabia's deserts.

Despite its deficiencies, including poor agriculture and a lack of water, important states—from Alexander the Great, to the Romans, to the final struggle between the Sasanian Persians and the Byzantine Empire—made efforts to invade or control the peninsula. In this environment of external involvement, several indigenous states—most notably the Nabataeans of northern Arabia and the Sabaeans of southwestern Arabia and Yemen—rose and became important forces in the ancient world, even contending successfully against Hellenistic and Roman armies.

Archaeological and historical exploration of the Arabian Peninsula, especially in Saudi Arabia, is much less developed than in most other regions in the Middle East. Difficult terrain, the parched climate, a lack of local interest and means, and a society suspicious of foreigners have conspired to limit such studies. Recent decades, accompanied by increasing national wealth and slowly changing attitudes among some representatives of the monarchy, have begun to reverse this lack of development. Since the late 1990s, the government has also started to consider its archaeological treasures as potential draws for tourists, although this industry is far more limited in Saudi Arabia than in other Arab and Gulf States, especially compared to Egypt and Jordan. The future will no doubt reveal the many mysteries that remain under the sands and rocky plains of Saudi Arabia.

BEDOUINS AT THE CROSSROADS OF EMPIRES

Arabia was not the primary or secondary site of any of the major ancient civilizations. Lacking major rivers, bodies of water, or sufficient rainfall for continuous farming, it did not have sufficient agricultural potential to host an advanced state. While some isolated local communities did establish permanent settlements, the fragility of the desert existence in an increasingly arid peninsula after the first millennium B.C. did not allow for the extension of these communities into larger political states. Unlike in every surrounding region, from Ethiopia to Syria to the Persian Gulf, no ancient empire emerged from Arabia. Northeastern Arabia, along the Persian Gulf, developed several small cities and markets, but none of these survived intact beyond the Hellenistic period, nor became independent centers of significant authority. The limited archaeological work in the region has revealed permanent Stone Age settlements, with pottery, agriculture, and rock drawings, primarily along the periphery of the peninsula, regions that have always received more rainfall than the arid interior.

During the earliest centuries of human occupation of the peninsula, the majority of the Arabs were nomads, desert Bedouins, rather than the residents of agricultural communities. Other discoveries have revealed the possibility that central Arabia, from 8000 to 1000 B.C., may have received much more rainfall, may have had rivers, and may have supported more extensive agriculture and sedentary populations. Without established urban areas, as more persistent rainfall could have supported, other than in limited areas on the major coasts, the early Arabs did not leave significant written, archaeological, or other evidence with which to construct comprehensive histories of their communities or activities before the rise of Islam in the seventh century A.D. Recent historical and archaeological research has revealed much about these coastal civilizations, including Dilmun on the Persian Gulf. Dilmun, in the vicinity of the present-day Eastern Province of Saudi Arabia, stretching from Kuwait to Bahrain, was an important trading civilization from the fourth and second millenniums B.C. Its merchants traveled the waters of the Persian Gulf and Indian Ocean, serving as intermediaries among the civilizations of ancient Mesopotamia, the river valleys of the Indian subcontinent, and as far as Southeast Asia. Dilmun later became a subject state of, successively, the Assyrians (eighth century B.C.) and Babylonians (seventh century B.C.), and figures prominently in the epic of Gilgamesh, the ancient Mesopotamian creation story. As far back as the ancient Greeks, the Persian Gulf was known as an area famous for pearls, but the Greeks and Romans had few additional references to eastern Arabia.

The Bedouin tribes of ancient Arabia were loosely organized around family, clan, and other related groups. Tribal leaders, or sheikhs, presided over collections of clans, and were themselves elected by family elders. To ensure survival in the harsh desert, sheikhs demanded absolute loyalty and obedience, subject to the counsel of other village elders. Defiance could mean exile into the desert as an outlaw, with death likely to follow shortly thereafter. Families drove their herds of camels, sheep, goats, and other animals to seasonal areas, chasing the sporadic rains and the temporarily green terrain that invariably arose after a deluge. The camels were particularly essential because of their ability to carry heavy loads, travel 20–25 miles per day, and survive one to two weeks without water, depending on the temperature, humidity, and availability of forage. Beasts of burden for Bedouin nomads, they were also used extensively in the caravan trade, hauling goods across difficult and arid terrain that would mean death for horses, oxen, or other draft animals. In emergencies, Bedouins could also eat camel meat and drink the water stored in the animals. Camel hair and skin, along with those of goats and sheep, made up a vital component of the tents used by the Arabs as temporary homes as they wandered the deserts of the peninsula in search of water and pasturage. While the Bedouin treasured their Arabian horses for their speed, beauty, and utility in warfare, their lives depended on camels.

The Bedouin made a virtue of necessity, regarding agriculture—which the land would not in any case support—as morally inferior to their nomadic ways. Although not technologically sophisticated, nomadic Arab tribes developed an advanced society in their particular environment. Tribal customs focused on honor, long-standing blood feuds, control over wells and oases, warring over pasturage, and refusal to submit to outside authorities. Raiding was an important political and economic activity, but remained limited; in most cases, raids would be bloodless affairs, taking movable property and livestock, but only occasionally resulting in open warfare or massacres. These behaviors coexisted with long-standing cultural traditions of hospitality to outsiders, contact with sedentary communities through alliances, and the importance of external trade through long caravans of camels that traveled through Bedouin lands bringing new technology and ideas. The Bedouins were not aimless wanderers, either, but instead alternated habitually between the same territories, following the patterns of rainfall, vegetation, and tribal tradition. In the summer, they might move into the cooler highlands, while in winter to warmer southern terrain.

While some Bedouin tribal leaders had significant extended clans, the paucity of resources in the deserts limited the size of these groups. More influential and powerful sheikhs, who controlled oases, agricultural communities, or a collection of villages, would often take the title *emir*, which can be variously translated as prince, chief, or leader. Beyond these positions, tribal justice, economic agreements, movements to grazing areas, marriages, military actions, and everything else devolved to the level of the extended family or clan.

Ancient Arab society shared other characteristics with their contemporaries. As with most civilizations in the ancient world, including the Greeks and Romans, Arab society practiced slavery, using prisoners of war and their families as family servants, agricultural laborers, concubines, and for other purposes. Raids on neighboring tribes were also a source of slaves. Slaves from wealthy families could be held for ransom, and those from less fortunate clans sold to other tribes. Wealthy Arab families also bought black African household slaves from the Sudan and elsewhere, viewing them as a status symbol. Slavery persisted much longer in the Arabian Peninsula, however, with strong evidence that it survived into the middle decades of the twentieth century.

Because of its geographic position between the river-valley civilizations—east of Egypt and southwest of Mesopotamia—Arabia did feel the impact of the ancient empires in its history. At the intersection of so much trade, warfare, cultural exchange, and movement of populations, even the forbidding geographic isolation of Arabia's deserts did not shield it from interacting with the wider world of the ancients. Archaeologists have discovered artifacts—coins, trade goods, religious items—in Arabia that reflect the region's contact with the Assyrians, Egyptians, Babylonians, Achaemenids, Persians, Hellenistic Greeks, and Romans, but only the latter three were able to establish long-standing political, economic, and cultural ties across the peninsula. Because of its geographic proximity, the Egyptians under several pharaohs did dispatch military expeditions into western Arabia, but did not establish long-standing ties or maintain occupation forces.

The Assyrians, Babylonians, ancient Greeks, and other civilizations had peripheral contact with the Arabs in the peninsula. From the ninth to sixth centuries B.C., for example, Arab mercenaries fought occasionally in Mesopotamian battles, incursions against which the Assyrians and Babylonians launched punitive expeditions into northeastern Arabia. In 670 B.C., an Assyrian army marched through northern Arabia, en route to the conquest of Egypt. Parched by the desert and raided by Bedouins, the Assyrians, perhaps hallucinating in their dehydrated state, believed they had been attacked by flying serpents and other monsters. Although the Assyrians demanded tribute from Arab sheikhs, their conquest endured only so long as their soldiers remained in the deserts. Future invaders during the ancient period would avoid the central deserts of Arabia, campaigning only in the less arid, and more accessible, periphery. While the Persians laid tenuous claim to the Hasa in Eastern Arabia, the Hellenistic states and later the Romans forged alliances with the Nabataean Arab state beginning in the fourth century B.C.

RELIGIONS IN ANCIENT ARABIA

Ancient Arabia, for all of its geographic forbidding, was a welcome frontier for religious diversity. Most Arabs in the peninsula remained faithful to their traditional pagan and animist gods, worshipping a variety of deities, depending on the tribe and location. Among those receiving devotion were gods of the moon and the sun, as well as the ancient Roman gods Jupiter and Mercury. Some of these religious groups followed the Greek and Roman religions, adopted through cultural and economic ties to the Greco-Roman world. Because of the physical isolation of many tribes, some even followed religions, monotheistic or otherwise, that were unique to their tribes or regions. Others continued even more ancient animistic traditions, predating the rise of civilizations in the Middle East, and focused on holy sites. Although there was great diversity among the animist cults, they did share some common features, including the worship of stone idols, circumnavigation of these objects, and a readiness to incorporate new gods and practices into their ancient ceremonies.

Whatever their local traditions, many Arabs, even the most isolated Arab Bedouins, acknowledged Allah—God—as a powerful deity worthy of reverence and at least occasional worship. A small monotheistic sect, known as Hanifs, worshipped Allah exclusively and there is some evidence that it was to this group that the family of the Prophet Muhammad belonged. In this environment of variation, Jews, Christians of every imaginable rite, ancient pagans, animists, mystery religions, Zoroastrians, and other faiths found ready converts among the isolated settlements and wandering Bedouins of Arabia's caravan-crisscrossed peninsula. By some accounts, the Apostle Paul spent up to three years in Arabia after his conversion to Christianity, most likely preaching to the communities of Jews. Many nomadic Arabs adopted several faiths simultaneously, practicing whatever was the prevailing religion in the region through which they were passing.

The ancient Hebrews clearly had ties to Arabia, and their early centuries as nomads reveal the close connections to the Bedouins of northern Arabia. Over the millennia, Jews and Arabs coexisted in the Middle East and Arabian Peninsula, as revealed through the mentions of Arabs in the Old Testament. Some sources place Jews in Arabia as a result of the alleged conversion of the Queen of Sheba to Judaism by Solomon around 950 B.C. Other accounts place Jews in southern Arabia by around 115 B.C., in the form of small Jewish colonies of merchants, as well as converts. At a minimum, Jews settled in Arabia several decades before Roman destruction of the Jewish temple in Jerusalem (A.D. 70), and perhaps several hundred years earlier. Living primarily in the Hijaz and Yemen, they played a major role in commerce. While retaining their religious uniqueness, Jews in Arabia assimilated into the local social and political system, speaking a dialect of Arabic and taking Arab names. After the second Jewish revolt in 132 A.D., even more Jews immigrated to Arabia, assimilating into the Hellenistic and Arab culture of the region. The largest and most important communities were in southern Arabia, where even some Yemeni kings converted to Judaism. The largest concentration of Jews outside Palestine after 70 A.D. was Alexandria, Egypt, itself in close proximity to the Arabian Peninsula.

Under threat by Ethiopia, Persia, and the Byzantines, all of whom coveted the lucrative spice and incense trade, as well as the strategic position at the southern end of the Red Sea, the kings of southern Arabia possibly saw in Judaism a neutral faith, unaffiliated with any of the great powers, as they desired to be. Never a majority, Jews nonetheless became a significant, disproportionately wealthy and powerful faith in southern Arabia, and remained so for centuries. Although by the end of the sixth century the Jewish communities were in decline in Arabia, at the time of the birth of the Prophet Muhammad they remained a significant community in the Hijaz, with representatives at every level of society, from merchants to Bedouin. In Mecca and especially in Medina, Jewish clans controlled fortresses and trading firms, and were among the wealthiest and most important families in the region. Most followers of Judaism in the peninsula seem to have been converts, rather than Jewish immigrants to the region from Palestine or other areas.

By the fifth century A.D., Christians, especially those of persecuted sects, began to flee to Arabia, a region beyond the control of Rome, Constantinople, and the intellectual center of Alexandria. Nestorian Christians, Copts from

Egypt, Ethiopians, and Greek Christians from the Byzantine Empire all attempted to convert the Arabs. For nearly two centuries, the Arabian Peninsula was a religiously diverse area, with individuals and communities drawn to a variety of different religions and faith practices within those denominations. Although some areas, especially the Hijaz, tolerated diversity, in other settlements religious conflict often led to bitter wars, as in Yemen, where Jews and Christians of various sects fought for dominance during the sixth century. Foreign powers became involved in these Arab conflicts, as well. The Byzantine Empire aided Greek Christians, Persia supported the Nestorians, and Egyptian allies encouraged Coptic efforts.

THE SABAEANS

The earliest independent state in Arabia was the kingdom of Saba, formed as early as the eighth century B.C. in southern Arabia and Yemen. Many scholars have linked Saba to the biblical accounts of the kingdom of Sheba, whose queen met King Solomon, established commercial agreements, and allegedly converted to Judaism. Solomon's kingdom likely did conduct trade with southern Arabia and the Sabaeans, making this meeting emblematic of connections between the Hebrews and Saba. Archaeological evidence shows that the Sabeans did have wide-ranging trade, extending commercial ties as far away as Assyria, and controlling shipping in the surrounding waters of the Red Sea. Their ships traveled throughout the Red Sea and into the Persian Gulf, trading along the Arabian coastline as far as the outlet of the Shatt-al-Arab.

The Sabaeans were also technologically sophisticated, and developed advanced agriculture and extensive systems for irrigation, including a massive dam at Ma'rib, to control the flow of water from the Adhannah River. For defense against Bedouin raids, the Sabaeans built an extensive network of fortified cities, even being called "the land of castles" by ancient observers. Although for centuries Saba, under a succession of distinct dynasties, controlled the valuable trade in incense and spices from Yemen, by the fourth century A.D. Saba was weakening and had lost most of its territory in the Hijaz. The collapse of the Ma'rib Dam in 542 A.D. accelerated this decline. Confined to an increasingly reduced zone in Yemen, in the sixth and seventh centuries A.D. the Sabaeans were defeated and occupied by the Abyssinians, Persians, and Muslims, disappearing as a state under Islamic occupation.

THE NABATAEANS

The Nabataeans were a rich, powerful, and well-led kingdom in the ancient world, straddling key trade routes and strategic terrain at the juncture between Africa and Asia. Despite their importance, they have received little attention by historians or other researchers, in large part because of the limited number of sources that discuss them. Only a handful of contemporary accounts discuss the Nabataeans in detail, and most of these come from the Greeks and Romans. Fortunately, the tombs and other archaeological evidence, especially the spectacular site of Petra, in modern Jordan, provide significant original source material produced by the Nabataeans themselves. Political developments in the twentieth century, including the Arab-Israeli wars, have made investigation in this area problematic.

In addition to the hostility of the land, one reason why ancient Arabia was not conquered by Alexander the Great or the early Romans was the strength of the indigenous Nabataean Arab state. From their capital of Petra, the Nabataeans controlled the lucrative caravan network and incense markets of the peninsula. Based on the wealth from their trade, and taking advantage of natural wells that provided fresh, sweet water, their capital may have held over 20,000 inhabitants. For over four centuries, from 350 B.C. to 106 A.D., the Nabataean state ruled northern Arabia, the Sinai, Jordan, and the eastern shore of the Red Sea. Independent, then allied with the Romans, then finally subjugated by them, their society was highly advanced. Not only did the Nabataeans manage lengthy trade routes, they also employed sophisticated irrigation in the northern Hijaz, minted their own coins, and incorporated aspects of Hellenistic, Aramaic, Roman, and Arab culture. Many historians and linguists also give the Nabataeans credit for developing the written script that would become the precursor to a standardized Arabic dialect, a written language that developed as early as the fourth century A.D., and would spread rapidly in the sixth and seventh centuries with the dissemination of the text of the Quran.

To defend their territory, the Nabataean kings developed a strong military that was seen by the Romans as worthy in battle. Despite their skills in battle, the Nabataeans earned a reputation as a peaceful kingdom, with little internal violence, no civil wars, and impressive diplomatic skills. The city of Petra experienced very little crime, a characteristic that assisted in the city's development as a commercial center. Although they had an advanced legal system, Roman and Greek observers noted that the Arabs litigated very little against each other, preferring to settle disputes through informal discussions. The Nabataean system of laws guaranteed private property rights, water rights, and other privileges for owners, another explanation for the durable prosperity of the society. Even their final incorporation into the Roman Empire in 106 A.D. happened peacefully, as the Nabataeans recognized their occupation would be lighter if they did not resist Rome's legions. There may have been some minor skirmishes, but the Romans did not make note of any major battles to conquer the Arabs, unlike the contemporary annexation of Dacia (modern Romania) by the Emperor Trajan.

The Nabataeans created a society that incorporated Hellenistic, Arab, and other influences to create a unique civilization. Originally seminomadic, the Nabataeans were Aramaic and Arabic speakers, who had extensive contacts with the Hellenistic states after the death of Alexander the Great, and also established commercial ties with the Hellenized Jewish Maccabees in Palestine. By the fourth century B.C., the Nabataeans were an independent and wealthy state in northern Arabia. Although their original tribal laws prohibited them—upon pain of death—from building houses, planting crops, or drinking alcohol, their transition from nomads to sedentary Arabs ended these provisions. Alexander the Great had intended to conquer Arabia, to gain control of its rich trade in spices and incense, but his untimely death in 323 B.C. forestalled this invasion. In 312 B.C., Greek armies sent by Antigonus, one of the generals who ruled the Hellenistic states after Alexander's empire, attacked the Nabataeans. At the time, this Arab confederation was mostly nomadic, but wealthy as a result of its dominance of the caravan trade. The Nabataeans also had an advantage over other nomads, in their ability to carve and sustain secret desert cisterns throughout northern Arabia.

Antigonus, however, did not expect to encounter difficulties, and sent a force of over 6,000 against these Arab "barbarians," as the Greeks called all foreigners. The Greeks won an initial victory against the Nabataeans, attacking during a religious festival, and withdrew heavy with plunder. Vowing revenge, the Nabataeans pursued the invaders and crushed them, aided by the sluggish movements of the Greeks, laden with treasure and overconfident in their superiority. After these battles, the Greeks and Nabataeans accepted an informal truce. Realizing the difficulties of waging war against the nomadic Nabataeans, who could disappear into the desert and strike unexpectedly, the two major Hellenistic states in the region—Ptolemaic Egypt and the Seleucids in Asia Minor and Mesopotamia—established commercial and diplomatic ties with the Arabs, and continued to fight wars against each other, each trying to expand their empire to take in all the lands originally conquered by Alexander the Great. In 88 B.C., another Seleucid king, Antiochus XII, made war against the Nabataeans, but lost his armies and his life fighting against the Arabs. In the aftermath of this victory, the Nabataeans launched a campaign of expansion, occupying Damascus and intervening in Palestine.

At the greatest extent of their empire—from approximately 30 B.C. to 40 A.D.—the Nabataeans were a powerful and extensive state. They occupied key terrain linking the Arabian Peninsula with the Mediterranean, caravan routes through the Hijaz and beyond, the Negev port of Aqaba, as well as the fertile lands of Transjordan. As early as 62 B.C. their kingdom entered agreements to accept the authority of Rome, paying 30 talents of silver to prevent an invasion, promising to avoid involvement in Judea, and agreeing to pay annual tribute to the Roman governor in Damascus in return for continued independence for the kingdom. Nabataea thus became a client state of Rome, allied to it but not occupied by Roman armies. Subsequent attacks by Roman armies in Syria in search of plunder soured these relations, however. Faced with Roman unreliability, the Nabataeans did not remain faithful to their status as a client state, and allied with the Parthians during the period of Rome's civil wars after the death of Julius Caesar in 44 B.C. Confronting a Parthian invasion in 40 B.C., which succeeded in occupying Jerusalem, the Nabataeans had little choice but to accept the eastern invaders. With the return of Roman forces, the Nabataeans had to pay a massive fine. Rome's more loyal client, the Jewish kingdom of Herod the Great, warred against the Nabataeans after 31 B.C., succeeding in occupying what had been Nabataean territory in Syria. The defeat of Antony and Cleopatra in 31 B.C., however, restored the balance in the region and unified the empire under Octavian, soon to be known as Caesar Augustus.

Realizing they could not continue to defy Rome, Petra's kings restored their ties to the Romans after this debacle. In 26 B.C., the Nabataeans allied with the Romans in an assault on the Sabaeans in Yemen, an attack that Rome hoped would gain control of the lucrative spice trade. Despite the assistance of a Nabataean army that accompanied the Roman force, the invasion failed, primarily because of water shortages, hunger, and diseases. A Roman army, perhaps as many as 10,000 strong, along with at least 1,000 Nabataeans and 500 soldiers from Judea, withdrew less than two years later. While some Roman observers at the time criticized their Nabataean allies for sabotaging the attack, the invasion of a distant and isolated territory would have been difficult under the best of circumstances. Had Caesar Augustus believed his allies had betrayed him, he would surely have ordered the immediate invasion of Petra and incorporation of the Nabataean territory into the Roman Empire.

The most famous and powerful king of the Nabataeans was Aretas IV, who ruled from 9 B.C. to 40 A.D. A client of the Romans, he ruled his kingdom for almost five decades, presiding over a period of unprecedented wealth and influence. King Aretas improved relations with Judea through marriages, and established better relations with Rome, after some initial conflicts over territory and the status of Palestine. Urbanization increased dramatically throughout Nabataea, including in the Hijaz city of Hegra. Aretas IV increased trade with the Romans, improved irrigation, and built major monuments in the capital of Petra, including an amphitheater, carved of rock, and a freestanding temple in the city center. Both show evident Hellenistic and Roman influences in their architecture, indicating the assimilation of the Nabataean Arab nomads into the urban Greco-Roman world. Most archaeologists and historians also attribute the spectacular Khanzeh (Treasury) building in Petra to the age of Aretas IV.

All was not well under Aretas IV, however. With the increasing use of the Red Sea, the overland caravan routes from southern Arabia began to decline in the first century A.D. Even more threatening, however, were worsening ties with some of the Herodian rulers in Judea, which led to years of sporadic warfare beginning in 27 A.D. The Nabataeans even briefly reoccupied Damascus, until Rome reasserted its authority in 44 A.D. under Emperor Claudius, restoring the borders that had existed in the region before 27 A.D.

Traditional rivals with the Jewish kingdom of Judea, the Nabataeans also assisted Roman armies in their suppression of the uprising of Jewish zealots that began in 67 A.D., dispatching 5,000 infantry and 1,000 cavalry to aid Emperor Titus. Remaining allied with the Romans in this war, in 70 A.D. the Nabataeans aided in the seizure of Jerusalem, the final blow in a counterinsurgency that led to the destruction of the temple in the Jewish holy city. Shortly after this period, the Nabataeans moved their capital from Petra to Bostra (Busra), a transfer that recognized the declining importance of the caravan routes through the old capital, and the growing importance of the agricultural base northeast of the Jordan River.

ROMAN ARABIA

When the Romans ruled many of the lands between the Eastern Mediterranean and the Indian Ocean, the province they named "Arabia" included parts of what are now Jordan, Syria, Israel, and northwestern Saudi Arabia. Most of the Arab peninsula, however, never came under their control, remaining the preserve of indigenous tribes and rulers. While the Romans considered the arid regions of the peninsula, "Arabia Deserta," as undesirable and ungovernable, they did respect the individual courage of Arab fighters and envy the rich spices and incense of the southwestern region and Yemen, calling it "Arabia Felix" (Happy Arabia). Chief among these spices were frankincense and myrrh, two products made most famous in the Western world through the biblical account of the birth of Jesus Christ, when these gum resins appeared as gifts brought by "Wise Men from the East" who came to witness the arrival of the Christ child (Gospel of Matthew, chapter 2, verse 1).

Despite remaining mostly beyond the control of the Greeks and Romans, the region of southwestern Arabia did develop complex political systems, and even more sophisticated commercial networks. Arabia Felix was a harsh land, bounded by deserts and containing no consistent sources of surface water. Although ringed by seas, Arabia to the Romans was an arid mystery, the source of much speculation but not worth the trouble to conquer and incorporate into the empire. Given that the Roman Empire occupied such far-flung and desolate regions as northern Britain, Numidia in North Africa, and the deep forests of Germania, Arabia must have seemed desolate to the Romans.

Southwestern Arabia was too distant for easy conquest by most of the ancient empires, accessible as it was only by sea voyage, but it did become well integrated into the trading systems of pharaonic Egypt, the Hellenistic states, the Roman Empire, and other ancient civilizations.

Unlike the rest of the peninsula, Arabia Felix was self-sufficient in agriculture, through a complex system of cisterns, wells, and other forms of irrigation. The soil was fertile, and with skill could produce adequate food supplies for the local population. Although there were zones given over to nomadic Bedouins, Arabia Felix was in the ancient world, and has remained to modern times, far more settled, sedentary, and agricultural than anywhere else in Arabia. By the late Roman Empire, however, the rise of Christianity decreased demand for frankincense and myrrh, used in large part for pagan rituals such as cremation and burial. By the sixth century A.D., southwestern Arabia became a contested territory, with successive occupations by the Abyssinian, Byzantine, and Persian Empires, even as its economic fortunes continued to decline. A mix of pagan, Jewish, and Christian believers by late antiquity, the region's importance became tied to little more than its geographic position and relative agricultural fertility.

Other parts of Arabia, including that of the Nabataeans, did not retain the long-standing autonomy of Arabia Felix. Under Roman occupation, the towns and cities of the Nabataeans joined the imperial system of roads and border defenses, and also had to adopt Roman laws. The legions were at work in the new province within a year of the occupation, improving its infrastructure and military preparedness, and beginning work on the Via Nova Traiana (New Road of Trajan) from the Gulf of Aqaba to Syria. Rome's governors built temples, baths, amphitheaters, and other symbols and conveniences of the empire. As a deliberate effort to Romanize the province, the Emperor Trajan named it "Arabia," rather than allow it to retain any association with its erstwhile kings. Petra became briefly the Roman provincial seat and residence of the Roman governors, but this changed to Bostra, the second city of the Nabataeans, also as a way to break from the previous dynasty. Petra remained important, however, and received ceremonial inscriptions from the Emperors Trajan and Hadrian.

The Emperor Trajan intended to use Arabia as a base to launch his war against the Parthians, in his dream of conquering the territories that Alexander the Great had seized. Even though this campaign resulted in his conquest of Mesopotamia in 117 A.D., Trajan died in the East with his dream unfulfilled, and Hadrian abandoned the newly conquered lands beyond Arabia. Emperor Septimus Severus (r. 193–211) favored Arabs during his reign, marrying a prominent Syrian woman and incorporating men from Arabia to important positions in the empire. Arabia became a productive and mostly peaceful province of the empire, providing soldiers, senators, and even an emperor,

Philip (r. 244–249). Philip, from the northern city of Shahba near Damascus, negotiated peace with the Persians and presided over the commemoration of Rome's thousandth anniversary. Although Philip's murder in 249 ended Arab ascendancy in Rome, Arabs continued to be indispensable in the defense of Rome's eastern frontier against the ongoing Persian threat in the third and fourth centuries. Although cut off from the spice trade after their incorporation into the Roman Empire, the former Nabataeans remained merchants, farmers, herdsmen, artisans, and soldiers within the empire, establishing a reputation as being excellent horse breeders and trainers, contracting with the Romans and local traders to provide cavalry mounts and agricultural draft animals.

Fortune did not favor their civilization forever, however, as changing trade routes and primary Roman roads bypassed the former capital of Petra. With the rise of Christianity, the indigenous polytheistic faith of the Nabataeans disappeared, replaced by the newer religious practices by the fifth century A.D. The advent of Christianity was also a major contributing factor in the decline of Petra and the caravan trade through Arabia, beginning especially in the fourth century. Although some Christian rituals used incense, the simpler funeral rites favored by the faithful did not employ aromatics from Arabia, a factor that concurrently contributed to the decline of Arabia Felix. An earthquake in 363 A.D. partially destroyed the city, adding to its decline. Shipping through the Red Sea, the Persian Gulf, and down the Tigris and Euphrates Rivers replaced the slower, more expensive, and more dangerous desert caravans beginning in the third century. After the division of the Roman Empire into East and West, and the collapse of the Western Roman Empire in 476 A.D., the former Nabataean Empire remained under the control of the Byzantine successors, although its distance from Constantinople left it far more autonomous than it had been under central Roman rule before the partition.

Increasingly using Greek rather than Aramaic, the Nabataeans of northern Arabia gradually disappeared into the broader community of citizens of Byzantium, subsumed as Christian Arabs along with coreligionists in Syria, Palestine, and Transjordan. With the declining prosperity of the late Roman period, and the weakening of the strength of Roman civilizations, Petra and other northern Arab settlements declined, and their populations resumed the Bedouin existence of their ancestors. Always precarious even in times of prosperity, the cities of the Nabataeans emptied during the late Roman and early Byzantine period. Many of Petra's temples, government buildings, and other structures, carved out of the sandstone hills that surround the city, survived the collapse of the empire, and the site remains important for archaeologists and tourists. In the aftermath of the Nabataean collapse, other regions and cities became increasingly important, including the new town of Mecca in the Hijaz.

THE RISE OF MECCA

The city of Mecca became a permanent settlement around 400 A.D. Prior to this, the site boasted a briny well, a dry valley, and something remarkable: a black stone meteorite, in the shape of a rough cube, approximately 12 inches in diameter. Islamic tradition points to Ishmael, son of Abraham and the concubine Hagar, as the founder of Mecca and builder of the first temple to house the black stone. The Ka'bah (cube, in Arabic) was unlike anything in the region, and as early as the second century A.D. the site appeared on Hellenistic Egyptian maps as Macoraba. Macoraba, or House of the Lord, became a site for pilgrimage and, because of its well, respite for caravans. Along with the Kaba, there were also idols to as many as 300 other gods. Although the shrine of the Kaba existed before Mecca, it was not until the early fifth century that a prominent tribe, the Quraysh, made its location important as a political and commercial center. Legend credits Sheikh Qusay, the original organizer of the Quraysh tribe, founder of the town of Mecca, and advocate of the Ka'bah as a site for pilgrimage, for this rise. Recognizing the centrality of the site and its religious importance, the Arab tribes accepted an annual four-month truce in and around Mecca to allow religious rituals and trade.

The Quraysh organized protection for the caravans that traveled through the central Hijaz, securing the continued north-south trade that ensured their own prosperity, as well as merchants from northern Arabia and Arabia Felix. Taking advantage of their cultural and tribal ties to northern Arabia, as well as their skills in using the camel in battle, the Quraysh exploited the initially modest attributes of Mecca to their fullest potential. Qusay also organized a consultative council of elders, established a tradition of service for pilgrims, and was the great-great-great grandfather of the Prophet Muhammad. The Quraysh developed extensive trade ties, traveling as far as Damascus, Egypt, Persia, and even into the Byzantine Empire to expand their markets and acquire goods for sale in Mecca, or to encourage pilgrimages to Mecca. They also instituted trade fairs, focused on local goods from Arabia, but also featuring merchants from as far away as Egypt, Persia, and Ethiopia.

Unsuitable for agriculture, distant from any usable ports, away from traditional caravan routes, perpetually short of potable water, subject to flash flooding, and possessing an unpleasant climate, Mecca became significant primarily because of its religious importance and the political skills of its governing tribe, which had taken maximum advantage of Mecca's modest attributes. As a result of the small flow of pilgrims that began in the fifth century A.D., Mecca did become a moderately important regional center for the caravan trade in Arabia, but it was not a rich settlement during its first two centuries. Unable to produce sufficient food to support its population, the Quraysh tribe, rulers of the town, encouraged trade and opened Mecca to commercial and religious visitors. The Ka'bah's initial importance was as a pagan shrine, with visitors to the site circling the stone, kissing it, making an animal sacrifice to the gods, and throwing stones at symbols of evil: essentially the same rituals adopted by Muslims in their hajj practices.

By the middle of the sixth century A.D., Mecca had become a moderately prosperous town in the Hijaz. Even as other regions, such as northern Arabia and Yemen, experienced continued declines, Mecca was increasingly at the center of trade and religious activity in western Arabia. Although not militarily or politically powerful outside the Hijaz, it was an independent and prosperous city at a time when the major powers that surrounded the peninsula—the Byzantine Empire, the Sasanian Persians, and the Ethiopians in Abyssinia and Yemen—were simultaneously weakening after decades of wars, internal strife, and economic decline. Mecca and its neighbor Medina, a much older and more fertile settlement formerly known as Yathrib, benefited from their relative isolation from these weakened regional powers, and were thus able, in the seventh century, to provide a base to unite the Arabian Peninsula under one state, for the first time in its history.

BYZANTINES AND PERSIANS

Arabia was at the frontier of several important civilizations, among them the Byzantine Greeks and the Persian Sasanians. The clash of these two empires in and near Arabia was also a religious war, pitting the Byzantine Christians against the Zoroastrians from Persia. Both states, however, governed over religiously diverse communities: Jews, Nestorian and Monophysite Christians, and animist faiths intermingled throughout the Middle East, along with the two official religions of the Byzantines and Sasanians. Although they never attempted to conquer the Arabian Peninsula, in the sixth century A.D. the Byzantines extended their forward defenses into the region. They formed a military alliance with and paid an annual fee to the tribe of Ghassanids, an Arab federation in the northern Hijaz, Transjordan, and Syria. In addition to military agreements, the Byzantines also entered into commercial treaties with the Arab tribes, purchasing dates and incense from them. Under the leadership of Justinian and subsequent Byzantine rulers, the Eastern Roman Empire regained its strength, building new churches and military fortifications in Palestine and Syria during the sixth century. Creating a client state in western Arabia was another example of this revival. The Byzantine Empire during this period faced a bitter rival to its East, the Persian Sasanians; thus Constantinople was looking for allies and resources wherever it could find them. In this regard, the warrior tribes of the Bedouins, especially those that had adopted Christianity, were logical auxiliaries for the Greeks.

The Sasanian Persians expanded into Eastern Arabia at the same time, taking territory and forming alliances along the Persian Gulf. In 225 A.D., the Persians invaded eastern Arabia, and soon after established the semipermanent occupation of key sites in the Hasa, the Persian Gulf and in Oman. In the late third century A.D., the Persians formed an alliance with the Lahmid dynasty of Arabs in the Hasa region. The Lahmids accepted the sovereignty of the Sasanians over northeastern Arabia, and in exchange received financial and military assistance to control the area, provided auxiliaries for Persia's wards against the Byzantines, and ensured the safe flow of the caravan trade through the region. The spread of Nestorian Christianity among the Arabs, at odds with the Orthodox Christianity of the Byzantine Empire, strengthened the agreements with the Sasanians. Almost until the conquest of the region by the Muslims in the seventh century, the Lahmid-Persian agreement provided some stability on the Sasanian's southern frontier, although the Persians had occasional trouble with their allies, and deposed the final head of the Lahmid dynasty around 600 A.D.—just before the rise of Islam. Persian Sasanian occupation of the region remained nominal, however, and for several hundred years eastern Arabia remained independent, free from direct control by foreign empires or other Arab states.

Unlike the long-standing Persian arrangements, Byzantium's Arab allies, mostly Christian tribes, proved of dubious military and political value in the campaigns against the Persians, and after a serious of rebellions the empire ended the arrangement in 629 A.D. Over a century of warfare between the Byzantines and Persians had devastated both states, culminating with the Persian conquest of Jerusalem, Syria, Egypt, and Transjordan in 614 A.D. The northern frontier of the Arabs came under the control of one state for the first time since Alexander the Great conquered the Fertile Crescent in the fourth century B.C. The Persians, as well, were frustrated in their efforts to find loyal Arab allies, and in 611 A.D. Persian forces lost a battle at Dhu Qar, encouraging them to end any efforts to expand into the peninsula.

According to some sources, including the Quran, the Christian king of Abyssinia (Ethiopia) also tried to bring Arabia under its influence. As an ally of the Byzantines, he could count on their naval support in the Red Sea. From its base in Christian and Jewish Yemen, occupied by the Abyssinians during most of the sixth century, the Ethiopians launched an attack into the Hijaz, perhaps even against Mecca, after 525 A.D., using Yemeni Bedouins, Ethiopian soldiers, and an African war elephant. The Byzantines encouraged Abyssinia to invade and occupy southern Arabia to preempt Persian expansion into the region. This occupation was short-lived, however. A smallpox epidemic struck the Ethiopian army, preventing its occupation of Mecca. The final blow to the Abyssinians was a Sasanian invasion in 575 A.D., which threw the Christians out of the Arabian Peninsula. The Persians stationed military forces in southwest Arabia, placed loyal tribes in control of the region, and allowed significant local autonomy. Although the Yemeni rulers did pay an annual tribute to the Persia Empire, the Sasanians tolerated Jewish, Christian, and animist faiths in their newly conquered province. Despite this liberal rule, Sasanian occupation would end a few decades after the rise of Islam, as the Persians fell, overwhelmed by the Bedouin storm emanating from the Hijaz in western Arabia.

CONCLUSION

Developing a strong tradition of independence at the tribal level, the Arabs would resist occupation and frustrate attempts at internal unity for centuries. The Bedouins, desert nomads of the Arabs, developed into fierce warriors that became skilled cavalry warriors, experts in swift raids on settled communities. While raids or tribal feuds could develop into long-running wars, such as those that took place in the Hijaz in the fifth and sixth centuries A.D., for the most part Bedouin fighting was brief and surprisingly bloodless. These tribes would remain autonomous, ranging over the deserts of the peninsula until one of their own, an Arab from the city of Mecca, would forge an Arab empire. This state would eventually become the first caliphate, a union of religious and political power under the authority of the Prophet Muhammad. Although loosely affiliated to the central authority of Mecca and Medina, the Arabs of the Hijaz, Arab Felix, and the rest of the peninsula did pledge their allegiance, for the first time in history, to one state, one religion, and one ruler.

After centuries of resisting foreign occupation, or at least benefiting from the difficulties that the terrain of Arabia posed for potential conquerors, the Arabs became part of their own imperial project, fueled by Islam and its impulses to jihad. The first and subsequent Arab Islamic empires, the caliphates, explored in Chapters 3 and 4, would not only bring together the entire peninsula, but would move forth to conquer vast territories in Asia, Africa, and Europe. This Islamic empire of Muhammad and his descendants would survive in various forms for centuries, leaving behind a legacy that still exists in the hearts of many Arabs and Muslims throughout the world.

3

The Prophet Muhammad and the Arabs (570–700 A.D.)

Central Arabia at the time of the birth of Muhammad was a desert peninsula, punctuated only by scattered oases. The region was populated almost exclusively by ethnic Arabs, speaking dialects of the same language and sharing many common customs. Most Arabs were nomadic and pastoral, as the arid landscape did not support many significant urban communities. The Arabs did not have a single state, integrated economy, or history of cooperation. Other than in the far north and south of the peninsula, they had created little physical or literary culture other than epic poetry, and did not have reputations for achievement in any of the major endeavors of life in the ancient world between the Mediterranean and the Fertile Crescent—warfare, architecture, written literature, or politics. Survival in the desert required nearly all of the attention and energies that the Bedouin could spare.

For all of the sparseness of its population and culture, the Arabian Peninsula nonetheless displayed significant religious diversity and disunity. Christianity, Judaism, Zoroastrianism, and many different types of animism and paganism held sway over the cities and Bedouin tribes of Arabia. In this theologically diverse environment, in which several brands of monotheism contended with many versions of polytheism, it would have been unwise to predict that, within a generation after 570 A.D., the entire peninsula would be united under one faith. Had anyone in the mid-sixth century made such a prediction, they likely would have projected Christianity, a rising force throughout the ancient world, as the candidate to win the souls of the Arabs. The remarkable life and achievements of the Prophet Muhammad, who inspired the Arabs to adopt an entirely new religion during his lifetime, and to create a vast military and political empire that would expand into three continents, demonstrate that in history, the unexpected can become real in surprising ways.

MECCA AT THE BIRTH OF MUHAMMAD

Mecca in the late sixth century A.D. was a settled merchant community, with its wealth and importance based on two activities: the caravan trade and pilgrimages to the shrine of the Ka'bah. Dominated by the Quraysh tribe, and fed by the well of Zamzam, Mecca was a regionally important center, and one of the most significant cities in the Hijaz. Astride the major caravan roads and trails in Western Arabia, the city was growing in population and influence, at a time when the traditional regional powers of the Byzantine Empire and Sasanian Persia were in decline after long centuries of warfare. Approximately halfway between the incense-producing region of south Arabia and the port city of Gaza, Mecca, despite its terrifying heat, absence of vegetation, and deficiency of natural resources, became a natural stop for caravans traveling through the region. Meccan traders established trade agreements and treaties of protection with the Byzantines, the Persians, the Yemenis, the Ethiopians, and surrounding Arab tribes, all of whom were willing to trade in and through the city, and refrain from attacking it or its caravans, in order to share in the modest wealth of its commerce and the opportunities to exchange ideas and information.

Equally important, Mecca was the site of the Ka'bah, a shrine that held a cube-shaped black meteorite, as well as idols for over 300 deities worshipped by the Arabs, representing all the major and minor deities of the Arabs and other groups. Considered a holy city because of this object, Mecca received thousands of traveling pilgrims every year, and profited from selling food, water, lodging, and other services to the visitors. The shrine become regionally significant, second only to Jerusalem in its importance for pilgrims in the Middle East. Even the well of Zamzam had theological significance. Meccans, and later Muslims, believed that the Angel Gabriel brought forth the spring to provide water to Hagar, the slave concubine of Abraham and mother of Ishmael. Ishmael, in turn, became the genealogical founder of the Arab nation, counterpoised against his half-brother Isaac, ancestor of the Jews. Despite its commercial and religious significance, Mecca remained a city with an unsettled appearance. Most of its residents lived in mud brick dwellings, or even huts made of palm branches, with only a few buildings of more durable construction, even as late as the lifetime of Muhammad. The city did not demonstrate any features that might predict its impending importance as the religious center of a new faith.

The elders of the Quraysh tribe ruled Mecca, supervising and promoting its increasing status among cities. As the ongoing war between the Byzantines and Sasanians continued, the overland routes from the Mediterranean to the Persian Gulf declined, replaced by a more circuitous route through Mecca. With the income from pilgrims and merchants, over the sixth century Mecca became less tribal and more urban, resembling a merchant republic more than a collection of clans. The four major clans divided the city into their respective areas, or quarters, but cooperated on community-wide issues, such as the renovation of the site of the Ka'bah in 635 A.D. In this event, Muhammad played a role, serving as a mediator in the resetting of the black stone into its original position. The four clans had struggled over who would have the honor of placing the stone back into its original place, and Muhammad proposed that each would send a representative to hold one corner of a blanket carrying the holy object. This Solomonic solution proved to the residents of the neighboring city of Yathrib (Medina) that Muhammad's wisdom merited their attention.

EARLY LIFE OF MUHAMMAD

Evidence about the early life of Muhammad is sketchy. He was born around the year 570 A.D. in Mecca, a member of the Quraysh tribe that dominated the city. Muhammad was not his given name, but is instead an honorific, meaning "highly praised," granted to him later in life. His true name may never be known. Muhammad's father died before Muhammad was born. His mother died soon after while he was still a young child. This led to Muhammad's adoption by his grandfather, and then uncle, Abu Talib, the head of the Hashim clan within the Quraysh. Muhammad was an intelligent and quiet young man, who participated in business and religious activities, but also enjoyed withdrawing to the desert for prayer and solitude, away from the commercial atmosphere of the city. He was exposed to the Christian and Jewish communities in Mecca, as the city was religiously diverse and tolerant. The Quran contains many references and allusions to these faith traditions, likely acquired during his youth in Mecca. Muhammad may have been a member of the Hanif religion, a movement devoted to a simpler faith around the worship of Allah, a traditional monotheistic deity among Arabs.

Although he grew up under modest circumstances, in his early twenties he married a wealthy widow, Khadijah bint Khawaylid, a woman 15 years older than he. Through his marriage, Muhammad became a moderately prosperous merchant, perhaps leading caravans in the Hijaz, while probably never leaving western Arabia. Some accounts indicate he led caravans to Damascus, in the Byzantine province of Syria, but the evidence for this is not conclusive. During these travels, initially as an employee of Khadijah and later as her husband and partner, Muhammad encountered pilgrims, merchants, soldiers, and other travelers, hearing Christian, Jewish, and other stories that he would repeat later in the text of the Quran. Without this fateful marriage, into a rich and prominent merchant family, it seems unlikely that Muhammad would have had the opportunity, and protection, to become the military and political leader of his people, and the prophet of a new world religion.

REVELATION OF THE QURAN AND DOCTRINE OF THE FAITH

The prosperity he found as Khadijah's husband allowed him time to find the solitude he craved, periodically retreating to a hillside cave near Mecca. During one of these sojourns, Muhammad spent the night in this cave, and received a vision. In this vision, the Angel Gabriel told him to recite a revelation from Allah. Over the following months and years, Muhammad received ongoing prophecies, revelations, and teachings from the angel, a collection of wisdom that would become the Quran, the holy book of a new faith. As a prophet chosen by Allah, the monotheistic deity revered by most Arabs, Muhammad dedicated himself to preaching to his fellow Meccans, urging them to discard their idols and pagan traditions, and return to the pure worship of Allah. The prophet also argued that the Arabs and all other people needed to look beyond their tribal, ethnic, or city loyalties to understand that they were all one community under Allah, and that this recognition would bring peace and equality to all.

The faith Muhammad began to promote in 610 A.D. became known as *Islam*, Arabic for *submission*. After converting his wife and a handful of relatives, Muhammad began to gain followers among slaves and poor Meccans, who saw the inequality of their city as a signal failure of the pagan religions supported by the Quraysh. Muhammad attempted to call Meccans back to the monotheism of Abraham and Ishmael, the latter the mythical founder of the city, and the worship of Allah. Not surprisingly, the city elders looked with disdain at Muhammad and his followers, especially the prophet's demands that Mecca abandon its support for idols and worship one god alone. Mecca could, and did, tolerate many religions, but it could not tolerate one that demanded the expulsion of all others.

Stripping the Ka'bah of its idols and expelling pagan pilgrims would have entirely negative economic consequences for the business environment of Mecca. During these early years of his ministry, Muhammad claimed to have made a supernatural trip to Jerusalem, known to Muslims as the Night Journey. In Jerusalem, he ascended into heaven with the Angel Gabriel and met Abraham, Moses, and Jesus, all of whom commended Muhammad's efforts and prayed with him. The site where Muhammad ostensibly rose into the heavens became after Muhammad's death the location of the Dome of the Rock, the Al-Aqsa Mosque, third holiest place to Muslims, after Mecca and Medina.

The faith that Muhammad preached became more developed during his lifetime, but the essentials began during these early years in Mecca. The core principles of Islam, or "submission to Allah," the name of the new religion, distilled into five central pillars. The first was the Confession of Faith, or Testimony (*shahada* in Arabic). This statement—"There is no God but God and Muhammad is his Prophet"—expresses the convert's belief in Islam and the teachings of Allah's Messenger, Muhammad. By making this declaration to other Muslim witnesses, one instantly became a member of the community of all Muslims. Conversion to Islam was a free choice, but converts could not repudiate their Confession of Faith except upon penalty of death.

The second pillar was prayer (*salat*). A Muslim had to pray five times daily: at sunrise, noon, mid-afternoon, sunset, and evening. Initially, these prayers were made facing Jerusalem, but the prophet later changed the direction toward Mecca, to reflect his disenchantment with the Jews and his acceptance of the Ka'bah as a holy site. Muhammad and his followers developed a simple ritual for these prayers, involving gestures and statements to reflect the unity of all Muslims, their submission to Allah, and the faith of the believer. In addition to the daily prayers, Muslims had to attend weekly Friday religious services at their local mosque, to join with their Islamic community, hear a sermon, and pray with their brothers and sisters in the faith.

The third pillar was the giving of alms (*zakat*) or offerings to the poor. For most Muslims, this tithe was equal to giving 2.5 percent of one's total wealth every year, although initially these alms were in the form of commodities (grain, meat, or other goods) given to the poor. A Muslim's first obligation was to give to the needy among his clan, then tribe, then broader community. Wealthy Muslims could give beyond this level, and many did. While during the first centuries of Islam most Muslims gave directly to the poor, over time it became more common for believers to donate to their mosque, to Islamic endowments, or to other organized charities.

The fourth pillar of Islam was fasting (*sawm*) during the lunar month of Ramadan. In addition to abstaining from food, drink, and sexual relations during the daytime hours, Muslims were also supposed to use the month to increase their prayer and reading of the Quran, as well as to focus on ending bad habits in their lives. The sick, the elderly, pregnant, travelers, soldiers, and the very young were exempt from the demands of fasting, but were encouraged to make up the time at a later date if possible. Muslims could eat and drink during hours of darkness in Ramadan, but were encouraged to do so in moderation. Throughout the year, Muslims observed restrictions on what they could eat and drink, always abstaining from pork, alcohol, blood products, and the meat of carnivores, such as dogs and tigers, and scavengers, such as vultures.

The fifth pillar was the pilgrimage (*hajj*) to Mecca, which all Muslims should complete at least once during their lifetime. This trip, made during the twelfth lunar month, included many ceremonies and prayers performed within the city of Mecca, including slaughtering an animal, circumnavigating the Ka'bah seven times, ceremonially stoning a representation of Satan, dressing in simple robes, and joining peacefully with pilgrims from all Islamic lands in rituals. Those who were unable to afford the pilgrimage or were too ill to make the trip were exempt from the requirement. Those who completed the hajj received the honorific title of hajji (pilgrim).

EXILE TO MEDINA

Muhammad's religious activity became increasingly unpopular with the Quraysh tribe in Mecca, as he argued against idolatry and tribal allegiances, and in favor of single-minded devotion to Allah and the community of all Muslims. With the death of Muhammad's wife and uncle in 619, the prophet's position in Mecca became increasingly unsustainable. Popular with the lower classes, who embraced his egalitarian vision of unity under Allah, but hated by most of the wealthy and prominent in the city, who benefited from the pilgrimages to the Ka'bah, Muhammad was also unable to gain many converts from the communities of Christians or Jews in the city and the region, a failure that was a great disappointment to him.

The city of Yathrib, however, was much more welcoming to him. Yathrib was very different from Mecca. It had fertile land, but also suffered ongoing internal conflicts. In 621, the elders and tribal leaders of the city invited Muhammad to settle their disputes, which threatened to bring a civil war. He agreed, and in 622 emigrated to Yathrib, a move known as the Hegira (Emigration). This event also began the dating of the Islamic calendar, starting at year one. Following the example of Muhammad and his Meccan followers, who emigrated with him, most of the leading citizens of Yathrib converted to Islam, and the city became known as Medina (derived from Medina't al Nabi, city of the prophet).

Muhammad directed the tribal leaders of Medina in the creation of a community pact, establishing laws, the rules of the faith, and allowing for mutual toleration between Jews and Muslims. He became the sole arbiter of Medina's affairs, and did not establish any formal structure or system of governance beyond his own decisions and the authority of the Quran. Medina thus became the first city to adopt Islamic law and practice, although these principles were still vague in many areas. The initial toleration for Jews ended within a few years, with the initial agreements serving as little more than a truce. Disappointed that the Jews had not adopted Islam as a new revelation within the older Abrahamic faith, Muhammad became increasingly hostile to followers of Judaism.

As a result of conflicts with Jews, Muhammad even changed the direction of prayer for Muslims. During his first years of preaching, Muhammad had directed that Muslims should face Jerusalem during their prayers, a holy city for all Abrahamic faiths. After he noted the Jews were not converting to Islam, Muhammad changed this guidance, instead revealing that Allah wanted Muslims to pray in the direction of Mecca. Beyond the conflict with the Jews, however, Medina served as the main base for Muhammad's plotting to return to Mecca, the most important city in the Hijaz. Although Medina continued to have internal conflicts, especially between Muhammad's followers and those who had dominated Medina before the arrival of the Muslims, these tensions did not rise to the level of a civil war, and the community remained more peaceful as a result of the coming of Muhammad. However, the Prophet did not willingly or permanently extend this peace to Mecca, and waged continuous war to return to his home city, interrupted only by brief truces, allowing him and his followers to make the pilgrimage to the Ka'bah.

RETURN TO MECCA

The Quran includes many encouraging calls to fight—to wage jihad (holy war) against Islam's enemies, both internal and external. In the context of Muhammad's exile in Medina, the primary enemy was Mecca, or at least the warriors of the Quraysh, who had driven out the Muslims and allowed pagan religions to hold sway in the city. From 623 to 630, Muhammad's forces launched attacks on Meccan caravans, fought several battles against the larger forces of the Quraysh, and gained increasing numbers of converts in Medina, Mecca, and the surrounding territories. In one skirmish, the Battle of Badr in 624, followers of Muhammad numbering 300 defeated a Meccan army of more than 1,000. Although Muhammad's forces did not win every battle, he did achieve more victories than defeats, and seemed to have momentum on his side.

Over the next few years, Muhammad's able administration of Medina and the simplicity of Islam gained more followers in the Hijaz, while Mecca faced increasing disruption of its trade and religious activities. After several failed truces, in 630 A.D. Muhammad marched on Mecca with an army of 10,000. Realizing they could not defeat the Muslim forces, the leaders of the Quraysh surrendered the city peacefully to Muhammad and he entered Mecca as a conqueror. Muhammad ordered the destruction of all idols in the city, especially in and around the Ka'bah, and Mecca became the second Muslim community.

Even after the occupation of Mecca, Muhammad remained a resident of Medina and kept it as his capital, from there engineering wars of unification, religion, and conquest throughout the Arabian Peninsula. With the fall of Mecca in 630, Muhammad became the unchallenged master of western Arabia, and soon thereafter the entire peninsula. Tribes throughout the region converted to Islam, or at least accepted the sovereignty of Muhammad. Marshalling the raiding prowess, horsemanship, and Arab warrior ethos to the concept of jihad, Muhammad created a Bedouin army to unite Arabia. His vision was to unite the Arab people under Islam and then to make war against the Byzantine Romans and Sasanian Persians, assuming they would not convert to Islam and submit to the authority of Allah, the Quran, and the Prophet.

THE ISSUE OF SUCCESSION

Muhammad died in 632 A.D. after a brief illness, possibly typhoid fever. He had achieved great things, with the western areas of the Arabian Peninsula united under Islam and the leadership of the messenger of Allah. The prophet had not, however, left clear instructions on the issue of succession. His only son, Abraham, had died in infancy, and his four daughters were unsuitable for leadership because of their gender. The two historical ways of selecting leaders—election or inheritance—thus confronted the new community of Muslims. Should the Arabs choose a new leader from the male relatives of Muhammad, or should they elect a leader from among the closest followers of the prophet? The Quran did not offer any direction on the issue, either. This fundamental question—the generational transfer of leadership—would divide the Islamic community in the seventh century, creating a permanent schism in what had been a remarkably unified faith.

DIVISION OF THE FAITH AND THE RISE OF THE CALIPHATE

After the death of Muhammad, the leaders of the Islamic community met in Medina to elect a successor. The gathering chose Muhammad's father-in-law, Abu Bakr al-Siddiq, to be caliph (successor). In addition to having been one of the first converts to Islam, Abu Bakr had also substituted for Muhammad when the prophet was too ill to lead public prayers. The position of caliph conveyed to Abu Bakr and subsequent holders of the office Muhammad's authority as battlefield commander, political authority, religious leader, and judge, but not his legitimacy as a prophet. The Quran and the teachings of Muhammad were to be the final revelations in history. Although he only ruled for two years, Abu Bakr was famous for his piety and battlefield skills.

One of his first challenges was leading the Muslims against tribes who had tried to break away after Muhammad's death. Following Arab tradition, these tribes had regarded their pledges of loyalty to Muhammad and his new religion severed at the passing of the prophet. The new caliph, however, insisted that Islam was not an ephemeral pact, but a permanent faith and community that required permanent loyalty. The Quran made clear that men and women were free to choose Islam, but could not leave the faith without facing the penalty of death. The centers of rebellion—Yemen in the southwest, and the deserts of the Nejd and Yamama in the south—quickly fell to the caliph's armies. Abu Bakr's success in forcing the tribes of Arabia to renew their pledges of faith to Islam preserved the religion and the Arab empire, extending its reach into areas Muhammad had not been able to claim. Even though it was brief, Abu Bakr's reign showed that the community of Muslims could survive the death of their prophet and leader. The first caliph had extended the faith into the rest of the Arabian Peninsula as far south as Yemen and east to the Persian Gulf, consolidated the office of caliph, and created a standing army to cope with the internal and external threats to the Arab empire.

CALIPH UMAR

The second caliph, chosen by Abu Bakr before his death, was Umar ibn al-Khattab, who ruled from 634 to 644 A.D. His rule corresponded with the first great expansion of the Muslims, as they launched attacks north into Byzantine and Persian territories. Although these attacks began as raids, through which the Arabs sought plunder, the weakness of both empires encouraged larger campaigns and wars of conquest. Two major victories signaled the beginnings of the new Arab Islamic empire. In 636, a small Arab army defeated a much larger Byzantine force at the Yarmuk River near Damascus, in the aftermath taking control of Damascus and Palestine from the Greeks. The Muslims took most of Egypt from the Byzantines in 640 A.D., occupying the capital, Alexandria, in 642. As in other areas, the local Coptic Christians welcomed the arrival of the Muslims after the high taxes and religious oppression under the Byzantine emperors. Islamic rule also meant an end to the conscription of Christians to fight in Byzantium's wars, a welcome relief to the Copts and other Christians throughout the region. In the Arabian Peninsula, however, the Muslims were not so tolerant, and in 640 Umar expelled the last Nestorian Christian community from the southern province of Najran.

The Arabs also continued to move North and East against the Persian Sasanians. In 637, another Arab force slaughtered a Persian army at Qadisiya, in southern Iraq, leading to the Muslim conquest of the southwestern region of the Persian Empire. Moving into the heart of the Persian Empire, the Arab Muslims continued to defeat Sasanian armies and occupied the Persian capital Ctesiphon in 638. Mosul and Babylon fell in 641, and the Arabs crushed the last large Persian army in the same year. The mostly Christian Aramaeans of Iraq welcomed the Muslims, as this ended their persecution by the Persian Zoroastrians. Through the course of his reign, Caliph Umar greatly expanded the Islamic empire, conquering Jerusalem, Syria, northern Egypt and most of the Fertile Crescent of modern-day Iraq and western Iran.

Umar's armies of Bedouin cavalry, mounted on camels and filled with the spirit of jihad, defeated much larger armies of Greek Byzantine and Persian Sasanian infantry and horse cavalry. Weakened by hundreds of years of warfare, the Byzantines and Persians were unprepared for this assault from the southern deserts of Arabia. Christian populations in Syria and Palestine welcomed Arab rule, as it freed them from the harsh rule, religious orthodoxy, and high taxes imposed by Constantinople. Under the caliphate of Umar, Islam was a tolerant faith. Christians, Jews, and those of other monotheistic faiths could continue their religions, as long as they paid higher taxes to their Muslim rulers.

CALIPH UTHMAN

The third caliph, Uthman, was less successful than his predecessors. Although his reign, beginning in 644, did oversee the final written compilation of the Quran, and the capture of the last Persian emperor in 651, he also presided over the first major partition within Islam, a division that would remain significant to the modern era. His caliphate also marked the end of Arab expansion. Although the Islamic faith would continue to expand in all directions, and Arabs would participate in many of these conquests, Arabs had reached the maximum extent of their exclusive control and occupation. After the late seventh century, Berbers, Persians, Slavs, Africans, Turks, Kurds, and other peoples would convert to Islam in large numbers and join the Islamic community as leaders and warriors, in many cases supplanting the roles held by Arabs in the generation that immediately followed the death of Muhammad.

A native of Mecca and a member of the Quraysh tribe, Uthman's family had been among those who had persecuted Muhammad. Many Muslims also accused Uthman of tolerating corruption and favoritism toward the Meccans. Anger against Uthman rose so high that in 656 a mob assaulted his home in Medina and murdered him. The new caliph after Uthman's death was Ali ibn Abu Talib, Muhammad's cousin and son-in-law, who had been under consideration in 632 to fill Muhammad's position. Some of Ali's opponents suspected that he had been involved in the killing of Uthman, since he had been in Medina and had been a rival to Uthman. Although there was little evidence for this accusation, these bad feelings prevented Ali from uniting all Muslims under his banner once he took the title of caliph. Ali's followers, who had long resented the failure of other Muslims to grant the caliphate to their leader, became known as the *shia t' Ali* (party of Ali), or *shia* (party), while the rest of the Islamic community called itself the *sunni,* or "people of the tradition." At this point, the divisions between the two sides were primarily over the issue of succession to the caliphate, rather than over religious ideology.

CALIPH ALI AND THE SUNNI-SHIA CONFLICT

The Sunnis refused to accept Ali as the new caliph. In 656, Ali defeated an army of his opponents near Basra, in what become known as the "Battle of the Camel," because of the camel ridden by one of his opponents. Even after this victory by Ali, his Meccan rivals insisted that the caliph should be Muawiya ibn Abu Sufyan, the governor of Damascus, a key member of the Umayyad tribe. Muawiya, who had been born in Mecca around 600, was a skilled battlefield commander and negotiator. His army, well trained and well paid, was the most professional in the Arab world. The Umayyads were Meccans, with a more secular and tolerant perspective on Islam, and Muawiya counted Christians among his closest advisers. Over the issue of choosing the next caliph, a civil war began among the Arabs, pitting the Shia who supported Ali against the Sunni supporters of Muawiya.

Realizing that he had many enemies in the Hijaz, especially among the Meccans, Ali left Medina with his followers, making his capital at Kufa, one of the Arab garrison towns in southern Iraq. He ruled the Arab empire from Kufa, although he was never able to control Syria, still under the control of Muawiya. After a series of battles and unsuccessful attempts at arbitration, an uneasy truce endured from 657 onward, with the Umayyads in Syria and Ali in Iraq. Ali himself was murdered in 661, however, by a member of the Kharijite sect, a group that opposed the institution of the caliphate. After Ali's death, his two sons, Hassan and Hussein, agreed not to press their claims to the caliphate, in exchange for substantial financial considerations. Hassan died in 669, and Hussein believed that he would become caliph at the death of Muawiya, another reason why he did not oppose the rule of Muawiya during the caliph's lifetime. Muawiya's reign as caliph was very successful, with his military campaigns taking Arab armies to the gates of the Byzantine capital of Constantinople in 668 and 674, although the Muslims were unable to take the city.

When Muawiya's son Yazid claimed the position in 680, after the death of Muawiya in Damascus, the civil war renewed. Yazid did not have his father's political and military skills, and was a notorious alcoholic—a serious disability in a faith that prohibits drinking. Determined to overturn Yazid, in 680 Hussein left Medina with 70 followers for Iraq, where his father Ali had gained many followers, to raise an army. In Karbala, in southern Iraq, Yazid's Umayyad army of several thousand caught and killed Hussein. This event, commemorated annually by Shia Muslims as Ashura, the beginning of their split from Sunni Muslims, began the permanent division of the Islamic world. The martyrdom of Ali and Hussein drove an irreparable wedge between Muslims, weakening the unity of the faith and the Arab people. Although the initial schism between Sunni and Shia was an Arab dispute, Shia Islam became increasingly popular in the Iraqi and Persian areas of the Islamic Empire, in some ways becoming a way for Persians to embrace Islam without accepting the distant and legalistic Sunni version, represented in the late seventh century by the Umayyads from Damascus.

One result of the civil wars between Shia and Sunni Muslims was the permanent departure from Medina of the caliphate. Ali had ruled from Kufa, Muawiya from Damascus, and later caliphs would establish their governments in Damascus, Baghdad, Cordoba (Spain), and eventually Istanbul. Even though the dynasties that ruled Islam were initially Arab, the power of the Arabs began to diffuse and absorb non-Arab elements, gradually weakening ties to Arabia itself. The continued use of preexisting Byzantine and Persian administrative institutions and infrastructure, the gradual conversion of non-Arabs to Islam, and ongoing conflicts within the Arab people also contributed to the dilution of Arab Islamic unity and power throughout the Middle East after the seventh century A.D. The initial burst of conquest during the life of Muhammad and his immediate successors did not endure.

UNITY OF THE FAITH: THE QURAN

Even though Sunni and Shia Islam divided in 680 A.D. over the issue of succession, and subsequently over more substantive religious issues, the two factions agreed on the composition of the key Islamic text, the Quran. Muhammad had not written down the Quran, but had instead recited the text verbally to his followers, who had committed it to memory, and to scribes who wrote portions of it during the prophet's lifetime. It was not until about 20 years after the death of Muhammad that the Quran took its final form. Around 650, Caliph Uthman organized a committee of scholars and followers of Muhammad, some of whom had memorized large sections of the text, to bring together and systematize all known suras, or chapters. The committee, made up mostly of members of the Quraysh who had known Muhammad or were related to him, met to create one version of the text, to prevent degraded copies from breaking the unity of Islam. The committee gave titles to each of the 114 suras and put them in regular order, from longest to shortest, except for the traditional first sura received by Muhammad.

The committee completed its work quickly and sent copies of the Quran, the first major work in written Arabic, to the principal Arab cities. Although some Shia claimed that the compiler had altered sections favorable to Ali, nearly all Muslims accepted the text of the Quran as holy and inspired, and this first version of the scripture became the only official version of the Quran. Although there remains significant debate on this issue, many modern scholars believe that the modern Quran is the result of subsequent transcriptions from this original compilation, with only slight modifications over the centuries in script. Questionable transcriptions were destroyed. Muslims considered this text holy in its original Arabic, and only in this form was it the literal word of Allah to the Arabs, and especially when recited aloud. Some Muslim scholars recognized the need for translation of the Quran into other languages as a tool for proselytizing, but others remained ambivalent about the practice.

FOUNDING OF THE UMAYYAD CALIPHATE

The Umayyad dynasty, building on the battlefield successes of Muawiya and Yazid, established their caliphate in Damascus. Subsequent caliphates came from the familial line of succession, rather than being elected by the leaders of the Islamic community. The Umayyads also established a council of tribal sheikhs to offer advice, but the caliph retained the final word. After the death of Yazid in 683, the Arab world endured several years of conflict and civil wars, with contending caliphates in Mecca and Iraq. The Islamic empire begun by Muhammad seemed on the verge of disintegration, but this disunity began to end with the rule of Abd al-Malik ibn Marwan, who led the Umayyads from 685 to 705.

After defeating rivals in Arabia and Iraq by the early 690s, Abd al-Malik began a period of reform and renewal to consolidate Islamic rule. He imposed Arabic as the official administrative language, replacing Greek and Persian, introduced new coins, reorganized the provinces of the empire, and began construction of the mosque in Jerusalem, the Dome of the Rock. Built on the site of what had been the Jewish temple, before its destruction by the Romans in 70 A.D., the mosque was at the location where Muhammad claimed to have risen to heaven to meet with Abraham, Moses, and Jesus. After Mecca and Medina, Jerusalem and its mosque would become the third most important religious site for Muslims. Abd al-Malik also replaced the old Byzantine and Persian administrative structures with a unified Islamic system of taxation, bureaucracy, accounting, and laws, derived from the Quran, Arab and Islamic traditions, and some legacy practices from the previous regimes of the Greeks and Persians. Although he was unable to recreate the elusive unity that had died with the Prophet Muhammad, as the Shia-Sunni split continued, Abd al-Malik did rule over an empire that was mostly peaceful, prosperous, and well-governed.

The Arabs ruled their empire as a warrior and landowning caste. Although the Arabs mostly respected the private property of those they conquered, they took possession of state lands and the territory of rebels, dividing it between those who had shown courage in battle. As the ruling class in the Islamic empire, many owned vast estates with thousands of peasant laborers under them. Agriculture, especially in the river valleys and high plains, became the most important economic activity. Surprisingly, given their experience with caravans, and the traditional dependence of Mecca and other Arabian cities on trade, the Arabs did not increase their involvement in commerce, relying instead on Greeks, Armenians, Jews, and other religious and ethnic minorities to carry out merchant activities within the vast Islamic empire. Islamic prohibitions against usury (charging interest) may have played a role in this, as well as the ease with which Arabs gained wealth during this period from plunder, taxes, and seizing the lands of their enemies.

MUSLIMS, CHRISTIANS, AND JEWS

With few exceptions, the Umayyads did not impose Islam on the people they conquered. With their traditional tolerance for other religions, as well as their secular skills in administration and trade, the dynasty did not pursue religious purity or jihad against other Abrahamic faiths. Christians and Jews, who made up the majority of the population in the territory conquered from the Byzantines, did not have to become Muslims to live in peace. Pagans, Zoroastrians, and other faiths not mentioned in the Quran did not receive the same forbearance, but there were few of these religionists after the initial rise of Islam. In some ways, Arab occupation was a lighter burden than that of the Byzantines. The Byzantine Empire had favored Orthodox Christianity, and had periodically persecuted Jews and Christian minorities, such as Copts, Monophysites, and Nestorians. The Arabs did not care what sect Christians preferred to follow, so long as they obeyed the authorities and paid their taxes.

Given the tolerance of the Muslims, at least during most periods, and the financial incentives to do so, many Christians and Jews did convert to Islam. Initially, however, this was difficult. The Arabs maintained their tribal affiliations for the first few generations of the Islamic expansion. To become a Muslim, one had to do more than state the shahada, or confession of faith. Conversion also required new believers to gain acceptance into one of the established Arab tribes as a client (*mawla*), essentially a form of adoption into the clan and tribe. A convert would also be expected to learn Arabic, if he did not already speak it, to be able to recite the Quran—a text considered holiest in its pure, original Arab language. Although these disincentives diminished over the decades, as the Arabs abandoned their initial self-segregation, it meant that the creation of an Arab Islamic empire did not always directly correspond with the expansion of an Islamic community, combining Arab Muslims with new believers from the conquered territories of the Middle East.

Outnumbered by the Christians and Jews over whom they ruled, the Arabs were careful to maintain their religious and ethnic purity. Rather than intermarrying and settling in as neighbors to the indigenous populations, to be eventually assimilated, in most areas the Muslims established garrison towns, such as Basra and Kufa in Iraq. The military encampments became the centers for Arab martial, religious, and cultural power outside Arabia, and became important posts in the preservation of Arabic language, Islam, and Arab dominance. As Damascus, the Umayyad capital, became more cosmopolitan, many devout Arabs retreated to these fortress complexes, or back to the Arabian Peninsula, to reclaim the purity of their faith and the traditional customs of the Arab people.

CONCLUSION

Although Mecca remained the spiritual center for pilgrimage, and Medina retained some importance as the original heart of the Arab Islamic empire, in political and economic terms the center of the Islamic world left the Arabian Peninsula in the late seventh century, moving to cities in more central, populated, and prosperous areas in the broader Middle East. With its indispensable role of the site for pilgrimage, one of the mandated pillars of Islam, Mecca was nonetheless diminished from its earlier days of wealth and importance. Even as it lost its political influence, Medina became a center for learning, with scholars from throughout the Islamic empire coming to the city. Its mosque, founded by Muhammad as the first worship center for Muslims, became a hub for the study of Islamic law and theology.

Within the course of two generations, the Arabian Peninsula rose to become the center of a new empire, based on its two key cities of Mecca and Medina, and then declined in political importance as the Arab center of gravity shifted to Syria and then Iraq. Under Muhammad, the region had united militarily and religiously for the first time in its history, but that unity was unable to survive many years after his death. Even with its political decline, Arabia, and especially the Hijaz, remained the emotional and spiritual heart of a new faith. Mecca remained permanently enshrined in Islam as the focus of pilgrimage, and Medina's importance in Islamic law and theology also survived past the city's loss of the caliphate.

4

Arabia and the Muslim Empires (700–1700)

Within a few generations after the death of Muhammad, the center of Islamic power and influence left Arabia for other regions. The caliphates, the political and religious dynasties that ruled the Arab world, rose and fell in other cities—Damascus, Baghdad, Alexandria, and Cordoba—leaving Mecca, and Medina, the birthplace of Islam, in relative political obscurity. Arabs from outside Arabia, as well as Kurds, Turks, and other ethnic groups, also became increasingly important in the Islamic community. Events outside Arabia were important for the region's political, economic, and military development, but these events were decided for the most part without involvement by peninsular Arabs. Never again would Arabia be the political center of the Arab world, but it would continue to hold a unique position within the community of Muslims.

Changes in the location of the caliphate did not have a significant impact on Arabia, however, except to diminish the territory's wealth and influence. Few of the caliphs had any interest in the Hijaz, except to maintain the accessibility of Mecca for pilgrimage by devout Muslims, and so kept their interference in local affairs to a minimum. Although the Arabian Peninsula was not a major battleground, experienced few major political struggles, and was no longer the strategic center of the Islamic world, it continued to play a significant role in the history of the Arabs and other Muslims. The religious, historical, legal, and cultural significance of the two founding cities of Islam—Mecca and Medina—guaranteed them a place in the hearts and minds of all Arabs and Muslims, even if the centers no longer were the political capitals of a far-flung political and military state. Another factor in the relative political obscurity of Arabia was that hundreds of thousands of Arabs had migrated out of the region, as warriors, merchants, religious leaders, and others involved in the spread of Islam in all directions. While the deserts of the peninsula had given birth to the Bedouins and other Arab communities, the temptations of the more fertile surrounding lands drew them to Egypt, Syria, Iraq, and elsewhere in the region.

MECCA AND MEDINA

Despite its political obscurity, the Arabian Peninsula remained important in the consciousness of the Arabs, as the center of the faith. In their observance of Islam, Muslims also encountered Arabia many times. Two of the five pillars of Islam, the fundamental instructions of the faith, focused in the hometown of the Prophet. The prayers of the faithful, repeated five times daily by the pious, were made facing Mecca. While no longer so important as a commercial capital, Mecca was the ultimate objective for pilgrims, with as many as 50,000 Muslims making the hajj every year. Medina also became important as a center for learning, especially in law and theology, with teachers and students studying in schools attached to the city's mosques. Muhammad's tomb was in Medina, and he had encountered his first mass conversion in the city, so pilgrims to Mecca invariably included both cities in their itineraries. Shia pilgrims also often visited the tombs of four of their imams that were buried in Medina, and some stayed to build mosques, schools, and other institutions in memory of their departed religious leaders.

In a sense, while the direct political and military power of the Arabian Peninsula and the Arabs decreased, the spread of the Arabic language, the mass movement of Arab people, and the export of a new religion magnified the historical importance of Arabia to a greater summit than ever before or since. As importers of goods and money and as exporters of ideas and teachers, facilitated by the mass movements of Muslims during the pilgrimage season and at other times, the two Arab cities of Mecca and Medina remained vital to the Islamic world, even though they were no longer the center for major political or military decisions. As the two places in the Islamic world where believers of every ethnic, racial, occupational, and political background could meet, Mecca and Medina also developed reputations for some tolerance for independent thought and free discussion, at least during the period of the hajj. Even more striking for the pilgrim was the mass spectacle of fellow worshippers, gathering by the tens of thousands, and indistinguishable from each other in their simple clothing. The shared devotion and experiences of hardship inspired the pilgrims, especially those who had traveled great distances and sacrificed their time and treasure to fulfill this pillar of Islam.

Medina, with its more temperate climate than Mecca, also became famous as a retirement community. Governors, generals, and merchants chose Medina as their final home precisely because after the eighth century A.D. it was a city almost completely uninvolved in politics, conspiracies, or military campaigns. Wealthy Arabs could move their riches to the city and remove themselves from the tumult and insecurity of much of the Islamic world. With this concentration of wealth, Medina developed into a city filled with retirement palaces. Medina also attracted individuals and institutions interested in selling to the rich—merchants of luxury goods, operators of houses of prostitution and other vices, and further locations that must have scandalized the conservative theologians that came to Medina to study Islamic law and theology. Outside the Hijaz, with its centers for pilgrimage and learning, nominal Islam was more common than piety. Especially among the nomadic tribes of central Arabia, conversion to the new faith did not always lead to an abandoning of older, pagan practices. Periodic campaigns against heresy and apostasy, launched against tribes whose Islam was in question, eventually consolidated the faith of the peninsular Arabs, so that by the tenth century the region was almost entirely Muslim.

THE FALL OF THE UMAYYAD DYNASTY

The Umayyad caliphs, from their base in Damascus, had difficulty controlling the extensive territory of the Islamic empire. Their state was an Arab one, with key administrative posts and the vast majority of positions within the military reserved for this group, especially the cavalry. Arab Muslims did not pay taxes, and nearly everywhere outside Arabia remained a minority. Below the Arab Muslims were subordinate classes in society. Those who converted to Islam but were not Arabs were known as the Mawali. These Persians, Kurds, Berbers, and others had higher status than non-Christians, but were under the authority of the Arabs, and there were strong social and sometimes legal prohibitions against intermarriage and assimilation. Unlike the Arabs, the Mawali had to pay regular taxes, a point of complaint that grew progressively more serious during the early eighth century A.D. Over the course of the eighth and ninth centuries, many of the poor Mawali converted to Shia Islam, attracted by the sect's opposition to the established authorities of Sunni Islam, who were increasingly unpopular among the poor Muslim and non-Muslim populations of the caliphate. Persians, especially, converted en masse to Shia Islam, identifying with the sense of persecution inherent in the faith, as well as in opposition to the strong Arab identity of the Umayyads in Damascus. Also during the early eighth century, the Shia idea of a Mehdi, or messianic figure that would return to rescue his people, gave hope to many in an atmosphere of discrimination and poverty among the Mawali.

The height of power for the Umayyad dynasty occurred during the reign of the Caliph Walid, 705–715 A.D. Not only did the Muslims during this period expand into Central Asia as far as Samarkand, and into India, their forces conquered Spain, and then defeated the Germanic Visigoths and their Hispano-Roman allies, in 711. Islam had arrived in Europe, and would remain a power on the continent until the twentieth century. In the years immediately following this expansion in the eighth century, however, the Umayyads began to experience serious trouble. Not only did tensions continue between Shia and Sunni, as well as Mawali and Arab: ongoing struggles between Arab tribes, costly wars, and a serious of weak caliphs signaled the end of the dynasty. In 750, the last Umayyad ruler fell in Damascus. Although the caliphal family fled to the Iberian Peninsula and established a new ruling dynasty in Spain, they did not return to power in the Middle East.

THE RISE OF THE ABBASID DYNASTY

The caliphs that replaced the Umayyads and established the Abbasids ended many Umayyad traditions. In 762, the capital moved from Damascus to the new city of Baghdad, in fertile Mesopotamia between the great rivers of the Tigris and the Euphrates. The ethnic composition of the state also changed. While the Umayyads had been an extension of the Meccan ruling classes, and depended almost exclusively on Arab Muslims for positions of authority and military power, the Abbasids were more cosmopolitan and diverse in their base of support. While Persians gained significant authority and often held key positions in the government, the dynasty itself remained Arab. The Abbasids emancipated the Mawalis, granting them equal rights with Arabs, and depended increasingly on professional military units manned by Turks, Persians, and other ethnicities. Although the use of the Arab language and self-identification as Arabs increased, the dynasty was more inclusive of non-Arabs.

In economic affairs, the Abbasids also made significant changes. Unlike the Umayyads, who depended primarily on plunder, taxation, and landowning, the new dynasty encouraged business activity, developing trade, building roads, and expanding diplomatic and commercial contact with non-Muslim areas. From their capital at Baghdad, the caliphs also encouraged science and education, translating and preserving many essential works of the ancient world and promoting universities and libraries. Baghdad became a major world center of learning, with a famous library and a vibrant intellectual life. For good reason, their rule, 750–1258, became known as the Golden Age of Islam.

ARABIA DURING THE GOLDEN AGE OF ISLAM

Despite the continued Arab identity of the ruling Abbasids, and the rising cultural assimilation of many tribes into Arab consciousness, the center of Islam had shifted permanently away from the Arab homeland. The political and economic capital of the Abbasid dynasty was Baghdad. Although still important, the great Arab tribes of the peninsula yielded influence and power throughout the empire to the settled elites: merchants, Islamic scholars, and bureaucrats of the major cities. The two main contributions of Arabia, Islam and Arabic, remained the common imperial currencies of the Abbasids, whose rule extended from Persia to Spain, and from the Sahara to Anatolia. The Abbasids were not able to control their empire for long, however, and as early as the eighth century some regions began to become autonomous, while still accepting the nominal authority of Baghdad: Spain (756), Morocco (788), Tunisia (800), and Egypt (868). In most case, governors of these regions declared that their positions would become hereditary, without launching a full rebellion.

By the late ninth century, the caliphs directly controlled only Iraq, with the other territories officially under their authority but independent in practice. By the middle of the tenth century, the caliphs fell under the control of their Turkish generals and Persian bureaucrats, becoming figureheads over a nominal state. Local rulers throughout the territory of what had been the empire continued to govern in the name of the caliphs, and imams said prayers dedicated to them, but this ceremonial allegiance did not reflect any practical executive authority.

The armies of the caliphate also changed, becoming progressively less Arab and peninsular during the transition from Umayyad to Abbasid. The cavalry that had swept out of Arabia during the seventh and eighth centuries was overwhelmingly Arab, as were the militias and other part-time units of the Umayyad caliphs. By the middle of the ninth century, however, the army transformed into a professional force, made up of mostly Turkish slaves (Mamluks) and mercenaries, whose lack of ties to local communities increased their loyalty to the caliph. These Mamluk units, based especially in Baghdad, were better trained and led than local militia units, and by the end of the ninth century dominated military affairs. Outside of Iraq, however, including in Arabia, local governors relied on local militias to keep pace, suppress low-level rebellions, and collect taxes.

As the various regions became increasingly independent, Mecca and Medina continued to be important cities in the Middle East. In 762, a descendant of Ali, who called himself "Muhammad of the Pure Soul," attempted to launch an uprising against the caliph in Medina, having failed in his efforts to do the same in Damascus and Jerusalem. This rebellion failed, but it tapped into the long-simmering resentments in the Hijaz, which having launched Islam and an empire, had been sidelined by Syria, Iraq, and Persia. Resistance and religious innovation found more fertile ground in eastern Arabia in Hasa, as well as in Yemen, where Ismaili sects, esoteric Shia groups, founded states in the early tenth century. The Ismailis incorporated elements of philosophy and Eastern religions into their understanding of Islam, teaching that for every verse of the Quran there were two meanings: the literal one and another known only to the initiates of the sect, who could acquire the secret teachings through study and dedication to the religious order and its leaders.

Ismaili groups established themselves throughout the Islamic world, including in Arabia. One Ismaili group, the Qarmatis, became dominant in southern Iraq and eastern Arabia along the Persian Gulf, forming an independent state under the leadership of their founder, an Iraqi teamster, Hamdan Qarmat. Supporting extreme egalitarianism, the Qarmatis shared property and, according to some accounts, even wives. Although they did trade, they also launched raids into other regions, attacking Baghdad and other cities, even pillaging Mecca and stealing the Black Stone of the Ka'bah in 930 A.D. They believed that the Mehdi would return soon and that they had to prepare the earth to receive him. Their community in eastern Arabia in and near present Bahrain did not survive long, and by the late eleventh century their state collapsed. Although elements of the sect survived until the fourteenth century, thereafter they were absorbed into the communities of mainstream Shia Islam.

THE FATIMIDS

The Ismailis were a proselytizing faction, sending missionaries to North Africa and other isolated areas of the empire. In 908, the Ismailis announced a new caliphate in Tunisia, choosing the Imam Ubaidallah as the leader of a new dynasty, the Fatimids. The new state constituted an alternate base of power to the Abbasids in Iraq and began to expand rapidly. In 969, the Fatimid caliph Muizz conquered Egypt. Egypt became the new center of the Fatimid dynasty, where they ruled from the new city of Cairo, built as their capital. Fatimid military and diplomatic power soon conquered Syria, Jerusalem, and western Arabia, so that by the early eleventh century the dynasty was the most powerful in the Islamic world. A Shia sect ruling over mostly Sunnis, the Fatimids were careful not to impose their heterodox beliefs on the majority of their subjects, and remained a small minority among the ruling classes, even in Egypt, the center of their empire and the seat of their dynasty.

The height of Fatimid power was in the early eleventh century, and in 1057 they even briefly occupied Baghdad. During this period, the Fatimids also controlled western Arabia, and continued to protect and guarantee access by pilgrims to the holy cities of Mecca and Medina. Their merchant fleet controlled the Eastern Mediterranean and Red Sea, conducting trade with India, the Byzantines, Western Europe, and Islamic states throughout the Middle East. Strong supporters of commercial activity, the Fatimids also encouraged more efficient agriculture in Egypt, making use of the fertile Nile to grow cotton and other exportable commodities, rather than just subsistence crops. This period marked the beginning of the end, however, as the Fatimid rulers faced the same challenges as the Abbasids had previously: the declining power of the dynasty, the increasing dependence of the regime on Turkish soldiers of dubious loyalty, and the isolation of the caliph from both the population and the levers of power. By the late eleventh century, the Fatimids decline became precipitous, and their last caliph was deposed in 1094, just before the arrival of a new invader from the West—the Crusaders from Christian Europe. The Fatimid dynasty continued to be important in Egypt, however, and several of their leaders returned to the throne, although not as caliph, until the great warrior Saladin deposed the last Fatimid in 1171, restoring the Abbasids to nominal control over the Islamic world.

THE CRUSADES, SALADIN, AND THE MONGOLS

In 1095, Pope Urban II issued a call for Christians to march on Jerusalem to free the Holy Land from Islam. His call, announced at a church council in Clermont, France, was successful, and began two centuries of crusading. When the first Crusaders encountered Muslim armies, during campaigns beginning in Anatolia and Syria in 1096, they encountered forces whose way of fighting, armaments, and worldview were at odds with their Western values. The arrival of the European Crusaders coincided with a period of political and economic decline in the Islamic world, with a decrease in trade and ongoing small wars undermining the cohesiveness of what had been a mighty empire on three continents. While the Abbasid caliphate continued, it was challenged by the Fatimids in Egypt, the increasing independence of peripheral regions, and counterattacking Christianity in Spain and Sicily. Constant rivalries within the Islamic world undermined the ability of the Arabs to resist these onslaughts, and accounted for the initial success of the Crusades and other invasions. Turkish invaders from Central Asia, who by the middle of the eleventh century had conquered Persia, had also begun to move deeper into the Islamic world.

Another challenge to the unity of the Arabs and other Muslims was the rise of a small sect of Ismailis, led by Hassan i Sabbah, who took refuge in the fortress of Alamut in northern Persia. Known more commonly as the Assassins, derived from their reputed use of hashish, these Ismailis used suicide attacks on more mainstream Sunni and Shia figures to establish an environment more favorable to their sect. Feared throughout the region, the Assassins killed hundreds of prominent generals, scholars, and political leaders who threatened their denomination or became too powerful. Although too small to rule themselves, the Assassins made every effort to prevent consolidation of power by any other sect or dynasty.

In this environment, the Crusaders were able to gain many victories, establishing new states in Palestine, Syria, and the surrounding territories. This occupation was temporary, however, and within a century the Muslims began to defeat the Crusaders, a series of victories that accelerated under the famous Kurdish general Saladin, who marshaled vast armies against the Europeans. By 1193, Saladin had reoccupied Jerusalem, established a strong state in Syria, Palestine, and Egypt, overthrown the last Fatimid ruler, and restored the unity of the Muslims under the Abbasids, albeit only during his lifetime. Despite these military victories, Saladin maintained trade with the Europeans, especially the Italian city-states, arguing that these exchanges allowed Muslims to arms themselves with superior European weapons and find markets for surplus goods.

The Crusader threat eventually faded, with the surrender of the last European redoubt at Acre in 1291. As the Christians withdrew, however, a far greater invader entered the Islamic world: the Mongols. Fierce warriors from the steppes of central Asia and the high plains of Mongolia, the Mongols under Genghiz Khan entered Iraq in 1258 and conquered Baghdad. Primarily a cavalry force, skilled in horsemanship and archery, the Mongolian horsemen overwhelmed the stagnating Abbasid caliphate. After defeating the weak Arab, Persian, and Turkish forces defending Baghdad, the invaders occupied the capital and began to plunder the riches of Islam, accumulated over hundreds of years. The Mongols abolished the caliphate and brought enormous destruction to the city, looting the great library and destroying the irrigation works along the Tigris and Euphrates Rivers. Iraq became a province of the Mongol Empire, detached from the rest of the Islamic world to its west. The Golden Age of Islam had ended. Although other Arab rulers attempted to restore the Abbasids or other dynasties, no successor states were ever as strong, as vast, or as technologically sophisticated, at least until the rise of the Ottoman Empire in the fifteenth century.

THE QURAYSH HASHEMITES IN MECCA

The dissolution of the Abbasid Caliphate in 1258 revived the regionalism and separatism that had plagued the Islamic world since the death of the

Prophet Muhammad. Arabia was no exception to these developments. Although Arabia had accepted the caliphal dynasties in Damascus, Baghdad, and Cairo, only the Hijaz in the western parts of the peninsula had ever been under more than nominal control by the caliphs. Because of the spiritual importance of Mecca and Medina during the hajj, caliphs had been forced to send military units to ensure the tranquility and accessibility of these sites to pilgrims. Regardless of the changing regimes that governed the Islamic world, the holy cities had to remain open and able to provide essential services to visitors, allowing Muslims on pilgrimage to fulfill their obligations.

Around 967, the Quraysh tribe reasserted its control over Mecca and the surrounding region. The leading members of the tribe took the title "sharif," and claimed the right to rule through descent from Muhammad. Various sharifan clans competed to hold this position, gaining it through intrigue, assassination, election, and sometimes open civil war. In a sense, the Quraysh were validating the Shia argument that leadership of the Islamic community should pass through the descendants of Muhammad, although the sharifs were careful not to claim the establishment of a rival caliphate, and remained firm Sunni Muslims. Far from declaring their independence, the sharifs accepted the nominal rule of whichever caliphal dynasty in Baghdad, Cairo, and Damascus or, after 1453, in Istanbul had the most strength in the Islamic world. Their flexibility in this regard ensured the continuation of their rule, but also earned them a reputation among the tribes of the Nejd for opportunism, a liberal approach to the faith, and excessive cosmopolitanism.

In exchange for accepting the sovereignty of the caliph and maintaining Mecca and Medina for Muslim pilgrims, the sharifs would receive annual financial contributions from the caliphs. This placed the Hijaz in an unusual situation; every other province of the various caliphates paid tribute, rather than receiving it. Wealthy Muslims from throughout the empire also made large donations to maintain the Ka'bah and mosques in Mecca and Medina, funds that flowed through the hands of the sharifs. At times the sharifan rulers controlled little more than the city of Mecca, but at other times their military and political authority extended to much of the Arabian peninsula. With small mercenary armies, alliances with nearby Bedouins, and the sanction of the Ottomans, the sharifs were in a strong position when not threatened by rivals from their family. Surrounded by slaves, whom they appointed to high positions, and with the wealth and prominence of Mecca and Medina, from the tenth to the early twentieth century, the sharifs were the most important Arab political leaders in Arabia, until their final supplanting by the House of Saud.

The city of Mecca remained subject to the broader events in history. Prone to flash floods that at times threatened to destroy the Ka'bah (1630 and 1680), Mecca and the Hijaz were also subject to periodic drought, famine, disease, and political instability. Vulnerable as they were, the sharifs remained financially dependent not only on subsidies from the Ottoman sultans, but also on the plunder they gained from sporadic raids into the Arabian Nejd. Some sharifs claimed authority over the Nejd, although their occupation of the region was never of long enough duration to enforce this assertion. These attacks on settlements, Bedouin tribal areas, and other populated districts outside normal control of the sharifs, did much to poison relationships between Arabs in the Hijaz and those in the Nejd. Raids, of course, were a traditional source of revenue for tribes throughout the peninsula, but attacks by the relatively wealthy Hijaz Arabs on the Bedouins seemed gratuitous to the latter. The Arabs of the central plateau began to see those of the west coast as corrupt, exploitative, and excessively cosmopolitan enemies, while the sharifs and their followers could hardly hide their contempt for the Bedouins they saw as isolated and primitive tribesmen, subsisting needlessly in a harsh and arid desert.

ISLAMIC LAW AND THEOLOGY

From the eighth to the ninth centuries A.D., Arab scholars developed several interpretations of Islamic law based on the Quran, Hadith, and other influences. Sharia, or Islamic law, was an intrinsic element of Arab society, and because of this it would be very difficult to isolate dimensions of these principles that are not based on religious thought and practice. The concept of the separation of church and state did not exist during the Golden Age of Islam, and only emerged in the Middle East in the late nineteenth and early twentieth centuries under Western influence. The caliphs during from the eighth to eighteenth centuries governed vast regions that encompassed many legal traditions, and so needed new standards to incorporate and assimilate populations of Arabs, Persians, Kurds, Christians, Jews, and Muslims, as well as people of different ethnicities and religions. Emerging as they did during the height of Islamic civilization, they were examples of the brilliance of the culture that emerged from the Arabian Peninsula in the aftermath of Muhammad's life.

In the cities of the Islamic world, councils of scholars of the Quran, known as ulama, began in the seventh century to formalize philosophies of law, and legal codes for managing criminal, civil, and religious conflicts between Muslims, as well as in relation to other faiths. Meeting at prominent mosques in the cities of Damascus, Baghdad, and Medina, the most prominent centers for the study of theology and law, they contributed many important writings and schools of thought. In addition to setting down the law, the ulama in these and other cities served as a countervailing force on the military and political leaders. In cases in which caliphs, generals, or governors acted in ways that the ulama believed were incompatible with Islamic law, they could pressure the leaders to change their policies or face condemnation and resistance from

Muslims. Of course, the caliphs could appeal to ulama that were more favorable to their cause, but even this course encouraged them to make allies from among the legal scholars and to act in ways that could be justified by Islamic law.

Over the course of these two centuries, four major schools of Sunni Islamic legal interpretation developed in the Islamic regions. Hanafi, the earliest, largest, and most tolerant version of sharia, emerged from Iraq during the mid-eighth century. Arguing that reason, individual preferences, and personal interpretation could play a substantial role in understanding Muhammad's intent in the Quran, Hanafi ulama argued that the role of the state in enforcing religious practice should be minimal, with most practices left to the wisdom of believers. Malik ibn Anas, a prominent scholar in Medina, developed another philosophy of law, Maliki, deriving inspiration from the Hadith. Placing more importance on following the Hadith whenever possible, and relying less on individual preferences, the Maliki school was less liberal than the Hanafi, but still did not advocate using the power of the state to impose religious doctrine beyond the minimum to fight obvious heresies or affronts to the faith. In addition to making major contributions to law, Malik was also a prominent teacher of the law, whose students would create their own interpretations using the tools of reason and understanding theology that their instructor in Medina had provided.

The Shafi'i school of law emerged as a compromise between the Hanafi and Maliki interpretations, agreeing that there was a place for individual preferences in areas where the Quran and Hadith were silent, but that Muslims were bound to follow its proscriptions when it was not. Founded by Muhammad ibn Idris al-Shafi'i, a student of Malik's, it became dominant in western and southern Arabia. The most conservative school, the Hanbali, was also founded by a student of Malik. Ahmad ibn Hanbal was a strict believer in the Quran and Hadith, arguing that there was no room for questioning or doubting the scripture and its most literal interpretation. Condemnatory toward other schools of law, Hanbalis provided the inspiration for what would in the eighteenth century become the most prominent and powerful religious and political movement in Arabia: Wahhabism.

TURKS IN ARABIA: MAMLUKS, SELJUKS, AND OTTOMANS

As early as the tenth century, Turkic peoples began to move into the Middle East from Central Asia, taking up service in Arab, Persian, and other local armies. Originally as mercenaries and slaves, by the thirteenth century many of the Turkish slaves had become masters, overthrowing the Ayyubid dynasty in Syria and the Fatimid dynasty in Egypt. After defeating the Mongols in

Palestine in 1260, Mamluk Turks from Egypt and Syria came to rule Arabia. For the Hijaz, however, this shift from rule by Abbasids to Mongols to Mamluk Turks made little difference. Too far from Damascus, Baghdad, and Cairo to be governed directly, Mecca and Medina remained under the control of the sharifs. Periodically fighting among themselves, the Hashemite families nonetheless exerted direct control over the two holy cities, regardless of which Arab, Persian, or Turkish caliph claimed to rule Arabia.

Ruling not only Mecca and Medina, but also the Red Sea port of Jeddah, the sharifs benefited from the extensive trade in the region, income from pilgrims, and annual subsidies from whichever ruler, Turkish or otherwise, that claimed to protect the cities for pilgrimage. During the fourteenth and fifteenth centuries, the Mamluk sultans began to station small military forces in Mecca, Medina, and Jeddah, to protect these cities and guarantee the safety of pilgrims, but also to collect revenues from trade. Continually seeking additional sources of revenue, the sharifs often attempted to collect fees from pilgrims, even though they had sworn to exempt pilgrims from official taxation. Aware of the precariousness of their position under the eye of the empire, the Hashemites in Mecca avoided actions that might be seen as rebellious against the Mamluks, but nonetheless exercised great autonomy.

The greatest challenge to Mamluk control over Arabia, however, came not from the peninsula, but from Western Europe. In the early sixteenth century, Portuguese merchants began plying the Red Sea and attempting to dominate trade with India. Vasco da Gama's successful voyage to India, 1497–1499, marked the beginning of regular Portuguese expeditions to the Indian Ocean, as well as their expansion of interests into the Red and Arabian Seas. The Mamluks attempted to fight these Christian interlopers, who raided Muslim cities, built bases in eastern and southern Arabia, and attacked Arab and Indian ships trading across the Arabian Sea. By 1515, however, the Egyptian Mamluks, outgunned and outsailed, had to abandon not only their lucrative trade with India, but also their control over the Arabian Peninsula. At sea, the Portuguese became dominant, while from the north another threat—the Ottoman Turks—overwhelmed the Egyptian Mamluks.

After defeating the Byzantines in 1453 and occupying Constantinople, the Ottoman Turks, who had moved into the Middle East in the early fifteenth century, began to claim other territory. Converts to Sunni Islam, they were able to gain the support of many Arab coreligionists and, in 1516–1517, conquered the Mamluk empire in Syria, Palestine, and Egypt. As a result of this conquest, by 1517 the Ottomans became the new rulers of Mecca and Medina, territory they would officially hold until World War I. The Ottomans vested their authority in the Hijaz in the office of sharif of Mecca, confirming the Hashemites in the positions they had held for half a millennium. By the 1560s, the Ottomans had extended their rule to Yemen, installing a governor over the province and stationing a small garrison to protect the production of coffee. Eastern Arabia, along the Persian Gulf, fell to Ottoman armies by the 1680s. Through their control of the Red Sea and the Arabian port of Jeddah, the Ottomans imported spices from India, which were then taken by caravan to Damascus via Mecca. Until the nineteenth century, however, the Ottomans did not have much interest in Arabia, other than ensuring the safety of pilgrims to Mecca and Medina, protecting Jeddah, and fighting against heretics and troublesome bandits. On most questions, the caliphs in Istanbul were content to allow great autonomy to the sharifs over the Hijaz, or to appoint local governors protected by small garrisons of Turkish soldiers and their local auxiliaries. Given the distances involved, and the difficulties of ensuring rapid communications between the imperial capital and far-flung territories, this was in any case the most practical approach.

Despite their minimal involvement, during most of the period, in managing Arabia, the Ottomans did adopt much of the cultural legacy of the Arabs. Following the example of the Mamluk Turks, the Ottoman Turks left intact the cities, religious centers, trade routes, and other institutions of the Arabs, rather then replacing them with their own. As converts to Sunni Islam, the Turkish caliphs took Arabic names, had Quranic verses embroidered on their battle flags, accepted that the Arabic language would remain the official tongue for law and theology, and even gave Arabic names to their warships. Arabs, like Persians and Kurds, rose to high positions within the institutions of the Ottoman Empire, and in many ways were indistinguishable from Turks. European writers during the medieval and early modern periods most often referred to Muslims as "Turks" or "Saracens," rather than differentiating between the ethnic groups. The Ottoman Empire adopted the Arab school of law, Hanafi, which had been favored by the Abbasids, and brought judges and scholars from Arab lands to Istanbul and other imperial cities.

DECLINE IN OTTOMAN POWER

The Persian Gulf region was outside the major developments in Islamic history after the death of Muhammad, other than through its involvement with Shia and Ismaili sects. In the late sixteenth century, the Ottomans conquered eastern Arabia, including the Hasa region. Their hold did not remain long, however. Yemen became an independent Ismaili state in the early seventeenth century, but it had never been a key province. By the late seventeenth century, however, especially after the Ottoman failure to take Vienna in 1683, Turkish power began to decline in its more important outlying provinces. The Bani Khalid tribe, which had been influential for many years, had expelled the Turks from the Hasa region of eastern Arabia as early as the 1670s, and even launched raids into Iraq. The Hasa region was majority Shia, and a constant source of difficulty to the Ottomans even when it was under their official authority. Movements for independence by local authorities were also strong in the Hijaz; the sharifs of Mecca had exercised great autonomy for centuries, but by 1700, this had become informal independence. The weakness of the Ottomans, as well as the indifference of other powers, allowed the Arabian Peninsula to be nearly free from major foreign intervention for the first time in many centuries.

Even during the height of the early Islamic empires, the caliphs at best loosely governed the Nejd. Poor or absent roads, dispersed tribes, few towns, and the traditional independence of the region were major contributors to this condition. Even more importantly, the lack of ports, rivers, or natural resources diminished the interest of the Umayyad, Abbasid, Fatimids, and other dynasties in the Nejd. During the rule of the Ottomans that began in the sixteenth century, the region was mostly left alone. In the deserts, oases, and dry plains of the region, Islam and the traditional Bedouin culture of the nomadic Sunni Arabs remained bound together. The tribes of the Nejd were little touched by the Persian, Turkish, and European influences that had made Arabs in the Hijaz and outside the peninsula far more cosmopolitan and worldly than had been the case during the lifetime of the Prophet Muhammad. As fiercely independent as their nomadic tribes were, the Bedouin Arabs of central Arabia would have been a challenge to control even by a militarily strong and politically unified state, and the Ottoman Empire was neither.

During the period of Ottoman authority, few of the tribes in the Nejd had much wealth, power, or status beyond their immediate district. In 1446, however, a new dynasty began its history near Riyadh, in central Arabia, with the settlement of Mani al Muraidi, the ancestral precursor to the House of Saud. Dariya, the enduring name of the settlement, contained several small towns and wadis, but was otherwise unremarkable. There is little known about the early antecedents of the Saudis, except that they were similar to other peninsular Arabs from the Nejd: seminomadic, illiterate, devout Sunni Muslims, prone to blood feuds, and dependent on camels, caravans, and combat for their livelihood. The rise of this new dynasty would shift the center of gravity for Islam, at least in terms of its political force, from the settled and urban Hijaz, to the deserts of central Arabia.

From their origins in the fifteenth century until late in the seventeenth century, there was little to distinguish the Arabs of Dariya from those of other regions. The rise of the House of Saud in the eighteenth century, however, would signal the beginning of a dramatic shift in influence in the peninsula: away from the Hijaz, with its heritage as host to the holy cities of Mecca and Medina, and toward the Nejd, an unknown desert region in central Arabia. From the desert, however, would ride fierce bands of mounted Bedouin warriors, who would transform the face of Arabia and, after several failed attempts to unite the peninsula, would unite the region under one dynasty. Although Arabia under the Saudis would never reclaim its position as the dominant voice in the Arab and Islamic worlds, it would nonetheless become an independent state for the first time since the death of the Prophet Muhammad. The rise of the Saudi dynasty is the focus of the next chapter, and will also become the central story in the history of Arabia after 1700.

5

The House of Saud
(1700–1902)

1700–1744

The Arabian Peninsula in 1700 was sparsely inhabited, poor in resources, and peripheral to the major centers of global power. Known to the West and to the rest of the world as home to the founder of Islam and its holy cities of Mecca and Medina, Arabia existed in relative isolation. With perhaps two million people, the majority clustered on the two coasts, Arabia was modest in its population and resources. While on its eastern and western coasts there were permanent settlements of fishing communities, pearl divers, trading outposts, and even modest ports, the remainder of Arabia did not merit much attention. Central Arabia in the eighteenth and nineteenth centuries was a vast, arid plateau—the Nejd—punctuated by isolated oases and settlements. The dominant political, military, and economic forces in this area were the Bedouin tribes, who controlled trade routes, provided protection for allied settlements, and raided those of their rivals. The major tribes of the Nejd roamed over vaguely defined areas, or *diras,* with control over water sources, herds, markets, and villages within the region. Poor and eking out a bare subsistence, the Bedouin tribes derived their main income from date groves and herd animals, especially camels, sheep, and goats, supplemented by raiding other tribes and more sedentary communities.

The extreme temperatures, poor soil, aridity, and lack of natural resources limited the interest of any external forces. None of the major powers was interested in the interior of Arabia in this period, except in preventing the rise of a unified Arabian state, and only the Ottomans and the British intervened, primarily in coastal Arabia. The primary interest of the Ottomans was in the Hijaz of western Arabia. As the custodian of the two holy cities of Islam, Mecca and Medina, the Ottoman Empire had to take seriously the security, accessibility, and services available to Muslims making the pilgrimage. Western Arabia, the Hijaz region, continued to be ruled by the Hashemite dynasty. The tribal leader of the House of Hashem held the traditional title Sharif of Mecca, steward of the holy cities. While nominally sovereign, after 1517 the Hashemites accepted the authority of the Ottoman Empire and ruled in the name of Istanbul. Except during two brief periods, under the rebel Ali Bey (1770–1773) and during a decade of Saudi rule (1803–1812), the Hijaz remained under the control of Hashemite rulers, as Ottoman governors, to the end of the nineteenth century.

Hasa, the eastern coast of Arabia, was during this period more closely linked to the Persian Gulf region than to the interior of Arabia. Although it had become an Ottoman province from 1550, in 1670 Hasa had slipped from Ottoman control. From 1811 to 1838, Egyptian forces under Muhammad Ali waged a war of conquest, technically on behalf of the Ottomans, but this campaign ended without a permanent reassertion of Ottoman authority. The most influential local tribe, the Bani Khalid, exerted significant influence in Hasa, but was never able to assert its authority as strongly as its sheikhs hoped, unlike the Houses of Saud and Hashem.

British merchants of the East India Company also had a significant presence near eastern Arabia. Having driven out the Portuguese in the seventeenth century, and the Dutch after the end of the Seven Years' War (1756–1763), Britain remained the sole European power with strong trade ties to the region. Basra, although an Ottoman provincial capital, was the main port for the East India Company, made more secure after the signing of the 1838 Anglo-Ottoman commercial treaty. The British had little interest in central Arabia, except to prevent raids on their mail, shipping, and coastal trade in the Persian Gulf. Britain also made treaty agreements with the rulers of Bahrain, Kuwait, and Oman in the early nineteenth century, strengthening the autonomy of these sheikhdoms against the threats posed by Persia, the Ottomans, and Bedouin attacks.

In the 1870s, the Ottomans made a concerted effort to reassert their authority in Hasa, dispatching troops and diplomats to the region. The local population, containing large numbers of Shia, welcomed the Turks, seeing them as more tolerant of religious minorities than the Saudis. The Ottomans suffered from serious disadvantages in the region, however. Distant from their primary bases in Basra, Damascus, and the Hijaz, deploying forces in Hasa was costly.

The British were a rising in influence in the region, and encouraged Kuwait, Bahrain, and Qatar to avoid assisting the Ottomans. Finally, the local tribes, Sunni and Shia, may have preferred the Ottomans to the Saudis, but even more preferred to be left alone, rather than be forced to pay taxes and accept foreign rule. Still, the revived Ottoman occupation continued, and Hasa remained under Turkish control until World War I, although this occupation was under constant pressure from the British and the Saudis, both of whom had designs on the region.

The Turks did not mount a similar campaign in the Nejd during this period, nor did the British. Without the involvement of outside forces, the tribes of the Nejd plateau were on their own to fight, forge alliances, and develop their cultural, religious, and economic future. Among the dozens of tribes were the Saudis, established firmly by 1720 in the settlement of Diriyah, near the city of Riyadh in the south-central region. A succession of emirs ruled over the district, each concerned with his own precarious survival in the midst of family feuds, assassination attempts, and attacks by rival communities. Out of this struggle in the eighteenth century, which saw the rise and fall of many leaders, the Saud tribe was able to emerge as the most powerful, through making a critical alliance. This alliance, between the tribe of Saud and the followers of the Wahhabi school of Islam, become the foundation for the emergence of Arabia as a united state under the House of Saud.

1744–1818

The two men who made this pact were the Emir (tribal chieftain) Muhammad bin Saud, and the Imam (religious leader) Muhammad bin Abdul Wahhab. Their agreement in 1744 committed the Saud tribe to the Wahhabi version of Islam, and promised in exchange that Imam Muhammad would provide religious approval for the struggles of Saud against other tribes. Although initially reluctant to forge close ties with the religious leader, the emir's wife encouraged him to provide sanctuary and adopt the Wahhabi version of Islamic unitarianism as his own. The two families established personal ties, and the son of Muhammad bin Saud married the daughter of Imam Muhammad. Muhammad bin Abd al-Wahhab was a purist, who wanted to return Islam to its simplest and most literal forms, following the Quran and Hadith (teachings of the prophet Muhammad) without hesitation, elaboration, or accommodation.

Muhammad bin Abd al-Wahhab had studied Quran and other Islamic writings in Medina, Basra, and Damascus, and emerged from this instruction as a fierce fundamentalist, devoted to what he saw as the original intent of Allah in the Quran and Hadith. A follower of the Hanbali school of Sunni Islam, the most conservative of the four major schools of Islamic law, he brought his learning and values back to the Nejd in 1742 and began to preach in support of an Islamic revival. Calling himself and his followers Unitarians, for their complete devotion to the oneness of Allah, they soon became known as Wahhabis after the name of their preacher. Although the term was originally considered an insult, the followers of Abdul Wahhab began to regard it as an honorable name and began to use it themselves.

Abdul Wahhab was especially critical of Sufism, a mystical branch of Islam, and all forms of idolatry. The imam violently opposed the veneration or worship of saints, arguing that this violated Islamic monotheism. The Muslim confession—"there is no God but God"—meant to Abdul Wahhab that true believers should destroy idols and shrines, avoid decorating mosques, and impose strict punishments, including stoning, for even minor infractions. Seemingly harmless superstitions, such as magical charms, were subject to Wahhabi condemnation and harsh punishment as witchcraft. The Wahhabis even opposed any special reverence for the Prophet Muhammad or his tomb, arguing that although chosen by God to bring the true faith to the world, excessive devotion to the founder of Islam could veer toward idolatry.

Advocating the strict enforcement of Islamic law—sharia—in all aspects of daily life, he hoped to return Arabia to the religious fervor of the early Islamic movement of the seventh century. Wahhabi Islam was egalitarian, arguing for the equality of all men before God, was theologically simple, and argued that it was legitimate for the state to force Muslims to fulfill the pillars of the faith, including ritual prayer, alms giving, and fasting. Abdul Wahhab provided the religious legitimacy for attacks on more moderate Islamic communities, encouraging Saudi warriors to kill those who would not renounce practices condemned by Wahhabism. Within this new doctrine was also strong antipathy toward the Ottoman Empire and its collaborators, based on the belief that the Ottomans had become decadent, were controlled by Westerners, and were no longer true Muslims. The alliance between Saudis and Wahhabis endured, even after the death of al-Wahhab in 1792, and was one of the foundations for the eventual rise to power of the dynasty.

After the agreement between the Saudis and the Wahhabis, the two forces united to expand the territory controlled by Muhammad bin Saud. From the Saud base in Diriyah, the alliance began to expand in all directions. Before the arrival of al-Wahhab, the Saudi dynasty ruled over a small territory, with nothing to distinguish them from dozens of other similar ruling houses in the peninsula. Their state consisted of three towns near the modest oasis of Wadi Hanifa, hardly a base for a powerful regime. The new religious doctrine of the Wahhabis, however, provided the Saudis with the energy, charisma, and religious legitimacy for a campaign of conquest, conversion, and assimilation. Enlisting other tribes and Bedouin groups in their campaign of jihad, they raided and occupied much of Arabia. Attracted to the religious simplicity as well as the implicit religious sanction for plunder in the call for jihad (holy war), many tribes joined the Saudi-Wahhabi cause.

The Saudi tribal leader after 1765, Abdul Aziz, forged an alliance of nomadic tribes that continued to expand its territory throughout the Nejd. Drawn to the success of the Saudi mounted warriors, as well as the simplicity of the Wahhabi faith, Bedouin throughout Arabia began to rally to the summons to jihad throughout the region. Under the traditional rules of the Bedouin, the Saudi dynasty collected 20 percent of all goods and valuables pillaged on the jihad. With these revenues, the Saudis were able to dispatch occupation forces to newly conquered territories, as well as to fund Wahhabi religious teachers (ulama) in each of their new districts. These ulama, backed by Saudi military strength, imposed Wahhabi rules: smashing shrines and tombs, providing instruction in their purified version of Islam, and punishing violators of their strict laws.

The Saudis faced significant opposition during their campaign to conquer the peninsula. In the 1750s, an alliance of tribes from the Hasa and the Nejd united to fight against Diriyah. While this conflict ended in a stalemate, other confederations continued to form against the terror of a Saudi-Wahhabi regime. In 1765, a force of tribes from southwestern Arabia marched against the Saudis, laying siege to Diriyah and slaughtering a Saudi force of 500 men. The Saudi capital held and the attackers withdrew, with some of their constituent tribes accepting bribes from Diriyah, but this assault nonetheless showed the vulnerability of the Saudis to a unified force of Arabs.

In 1765, Muhammad ibn Saud died, and was succeeded as emir of Diriyah by his son, Abd al-Aziz. After surviving the siege of that year, the Saudi dynasty quickly regained its status as the most powerful Arab state in the Nejd. Riyadh, a flourishing trading center, fell to the Saudis in 1773, establishing their state as dominant in central and eastern Arabia. In addition to taking their share of plunder, the Saudi-Wahhabi state insisted on collecting the zakat, or Muslim tithe, as a formal tax on all cities, settlements, and tribes under their authority. These funds allowed the Wahhabis to control all charitable activities, fund mosques, and ensure the religious and political reliability of recipients of the assistance.

Strengthened by these financial resources, the Saudi state continued to grow in influence. Attempts in the 1770s and 1780s to organize military campaigns against their power did not succeed, remaining limited to sporadic raids on outlying villages. By 1790, the Saudi-Wahhabi union had consolidated its political, military, and economic stranglehold over central Arabia, and had begun a major offensive into the Hasa. This new campaign confronted distinct challenges, however. Unlike the Nejd, which had been Sunni Muslim long before the rise of the Wahhabi reformist movement, coastal Arabia was mostly Shia. Resistance here lasted several years, until the Saudis finally consolidated their occupation of the territory by 1793.

Throughout their domain, the Saudis implemented several important reforms that helped centralize their power. The dynasty gradually replaced local emirs in newly conquered territory with members of their extended family, or those of proven loyalty. The Saudis increasingly relocated to Diriyah, forcibly or voluntarily, family members of important Bedouin tribes, thereby holding them as implicit hostages to the good behavior of their home villages. The Saudis imposed their own, Wahhabi-inspired, legal system throughout the Nejd, replacing the traditional tribal justice and its cycle of revenge and personal obligations. To maintain control over distant towns and oases, as well as to enforce bans on internal raiding and feuds within their realm, the Saudis built garrison fortresses, manned with hundreds of loyal fighters during periods of conflict, and more modest forces when times were quiet.

Although the standing army of the Saudis was relatively modest—fewer than one thousand soldiers during the eighteenth century—the available manpower during military campaigns was much greater. Every able-bodied male was subject to military service during periods of official jihad, although in practice local communities only had to fill quotas for each major operation, rather than suffer the dislocation of a full mobilization. Long wars were unusual, with most campaign seasons lasting a month or less. The precarious environment, as well as tradition, did not allow for longer wars, unless the emir offered solemn guarantees of abundant plunder. Soldiers called to the Saudi cause had to provide everything they needed for battle: mounts, arms, and provisions, as part of their obligations to the emir. Although the Saudi army in the eighteenth century did have some small firearms, primarily pistols, most of its weaponry was edged: swords, pikes, and daggers. Nearly all warriors rode horses, although small units of infantry and camel troops were occasionally used. Because of its composition, as well as its ad hoc nature, the Saudi army was not capable of fighting extended campaigns, long sieges, or wars at a great distance from the Nejd.

Feeling threatened by the rising power to his east, in 1790 the sharif of Mecca, Ghalib ibn Musaid, launched a punitive expedition against the Saudis, with a force of 10,000 soldiers. This invasion failed, as the Meccan units lost troops to raids and the austere desert climate, failed to take important fortified cities, and began to suffer from extended lines of communication. The Meccans were unable to devote all of their forces to an extended campaign against the Saudis, as the threat of an Ottoman invasion of the Hijaz remained a serious possibility. Officially a subject of the Ottomans, and host to small Turkish garrisons, the sharif had to be concerned that his sovereign might reassert direct rule over the region.

Alarmed by this rising power in the Arabian Peninsula, in 1796 the Ottoman Empire launched a punitive expedition against the House of Saud, an attack that failed miserably. In 1798, the Meccans launched another invasion of the Saudi heartland, and once again met defeat. Subsequent efforts by the Ottomans to support other raids and invasions also did not flourish, and by 1800, Saudi forces had taken over nearly all of the Nejd, as well as the Hasa. In 1802, the Saudi-Wahhabis sacked Karbala, sacred city of Shia Muslims, destroying holy shrines and the tomb of Hussein, one of the founders of the sect. The Saudis also approached Najaf, another city holy to Shia Muslims, but did not pursue this assault. Although a tactical success, the attack on Karbala convinced the Ottomans that the Saudis were a threat to regional peace. In the short run, however, the Saudis were able to build on the success of the Karbala attack, using the funds they looted from the holy city to sponsor raids deep into Iraq and Syria. That same year, Abdul Aziz died, succeeded by his son Saud, who continued his father's aggressive military campaigns. Expanding West, in 1803 the Saudi occupied and looted Mecca, destroying images, shrines, tombs, and other objects they regarded as tempting Muslims to idolatry.

In their occupation of Mecca, the Saudis introduced strict Wahhabism, as they had done elsewhere. Viewing their success as a sign of Allah's approval, they attempted to transform the Hijaz into what they believed was the original intent of the Prophet Muhammad, as written in the Quran and Hadith. Unlike in the deserts of the Nejd, where these rules did not require much adaptation, conditions in Mecca were different. The birthplace of Muhammad had, over the years of control by the sharifs, become a cosmopolitan center. Alcohol, prostitution, homosexuality, and tolerance for other faiths had become commonplace. Not surprisingly, the Wahhabis launched a campaign to end these practices, liberally employing the death penalty and other forms of physical punishment to purify Mecca of what they saw as idolatry, immorality, and violations of Islamic law. The Saudis also expelled the remaining Turkish garrisons, dismissed Turkish bureaucrats from the positions, and prohibited imams of local mosques from offering prayers on behalf of the Ottoman sultan during Friday services.

The conquest of Mecca and Medina, along with previous actions of the Saudis, angered the Ottomans, still officially sovereign and custodian over the two holy cities. In 1803, the Ottomans launched a small expedition against the Saudis, and succeeded in expelling them from Mecca and Medina. The Saudis returned in 1805, after the withdrawal of Ottoman forces, and reoccupied the Hijaz. By 1810, they once again controlled nearly the entire peninsula. Even the few independent states along the Persian Gulf, including Kuwait and Bahrain, paid tribute to Diriyah. Although powerful on the surface, the Saudis faced three significant threats to their reign. First, one of the greatest appeals they could make to Bedouin tribes was the possibility of pillage. With almost all of Arabia under their control, the Saudis had few targets available to offer for plunder. Second, resentment against the strict Wahhabi rules continued

within many regions, with tribal leaders ready to support any realistic opportunity to overthrow the puritanical Unitarians. Finally, for all of its success,
the Saudi-Wahhabi state was weak in comparison to the greatest power in the
region: the Ottoman Empire and its strongest province, Egypt.

Lacking a modern standing army, an effective communications system, popularity among its occupied populations, or a trained civil service, the Saudis
began to experience fraying on the periphery of their state. Along the Gulf
Coast, near Yemen, and in the Hijaz, Saudi rule was increasingly ephemeral,
enduring only during periods of occupation. Their raids into Iraq, Syria, and
other regions had also proved strategic failures. While successful in garnering
plunder for Diriyah and its allied Bedouins, these attacks had alienated Muslims throughout the Middle East. With the decrease in available plunder, the
Saudis had to devote an increasing number of campaigns to crushing internal
rebellions, rather than attacking new areas. The distinctive brand of Wahhabi
Islam also restricted economic growth, as exemplified by the 1810 ban on trade
with non-Wahhabis. For the Hijaz and Hasa, territories that had flourished
through commerce, these restrictions were additional reasons to be alienated
from Diriyah. Mecca and Medina suffered from massive decreases in pilgrims,
as the Wahhabis imposed so many restrictions on the hajj that the local economy of the Hijaz, deprived of income from trade, as well, began to collapse.

Istanbul encouraged the Egyptian ruler Muhammad Ali (also known as
Mehmet Ali) to take action. In 1809, Muhammad began to gather his forces,
hiring mercenaries from the Ottoman Empire and drawing recruits with the
promise to expel the Wahhabis from the holy cities. An ethnic Albanian who
commanded an army of mixed nationalities, Muhammad was an effective military and political leader. Among his forces were Albanians, Turks, Egyptians,
and even European mercenaries who had served with Napoleon. Muhammad also sent modern artillery, some of it abandoned by the French in 1799,
with his army. Encouraged by the potential wealth of the Hijaz, and hoping to
raise his stature with Muslims worldwide, he was enthusiastic about the campaign. Although a vassal of the Ottomans, he hoped to use his base of power
in Egypt to establish an independent state. Muhammad formed an alliance
with the sharifan forces and dispatched his fleet in 1811. Before dispatching
his forces, Muhammad held a reception for the Mamluks, the fearsome European warriors that had dominated Egyptian military and political affairs for
centuries, and slaughtered their leaders. With this potentially rebellious force
destroyed, he ordered his army to Arabia.

In 1812, Egyptian forces landed in Jeddah, the main port city in the Hijaz,
and overwhelmed the Saudis. In 1813, Muhammad Ali's forces expelled
the Saudis from Mecca and Medina and took control of the coastal Hijaz region. Although the Saudis attempted to launch counterattacks, Muhammad

retained control over the Hijaz. At this point, Muhammad made some major errors. Although his success in the Hijaz had depended on the alliance with Sharif Ghalib, in 1813 Muhammad had him arrested, and then placed a more pliable leader in charge of Mecca. The Egyptian leader even appointed a Scottish mercenary, Thomas Keith, as acting governor over Medina, an action that was anathema to the devout Muslims in the territory. Hoping to control Mecca's lucrative revenues from trade and spending by pilgrims, Muhammad succeeded in alienating much of the local population through his heavy hand. These ill-advised actions led to a simmering rebellion, forcing Muhammad to reverse some of his efforts. He lowered taxes, provided more charity to the poor of the region, and took other measures that minimized resistance to Egyptian rule.

After the loss of the Hijaz, and the shame associated with being expelled from the holy cities of Mecca and Medina, Saudi decline continued. After the death of Saud in 1814 and the rise to power of his son, Abdullah, the Saud dynasty experienced a host of troubles. Having lost all their territorial gains outside the Nejd, they faced a threat to their survival as a state. In late 1814, Muhammad launched a major offensive into the Nejd, defeating the Saudi main force in January 1815. At this point, Muhammad Ali returned to Egypt, leaving his son Tusun to continue the war against the Saudis. Unable to achieve a final victory, and with his communication lines to the Hijaz stretched thin across the deserts of Arabia, Tusun agreed to a truce and withdrew in late 1815.

Unhappy with this result, in 1816, Muhammad Ali relieved Tusun from his command and revived his campaign in Arabia. Tusun's replacement was Muhammad's stepson Ibrahim, whom the Egyptian leader ordered to launch a final campaign to destroy the Saudi-Wahhabi kingdom. The new commander brought with him modern French artillery, as well as French and Italian military advisers. After building his forces in Medina, and gaining popularity through ending the mandatory payment of the zakat tithe, Ibrahim began to march east. Throughout 1816 and 1817, Ibrahim fought against the Saudis, gaining support from tribes in the Nejd and surrounding areas, many of whom had chafed at Saudi taxes, forced military service, and strict Wahhabism. By late 1817, the Saudi emir, Abdullah, had lost all of his territory, except for Diriyah and the surrounding tribal areas. Ibrahim's forces reached Diriyah in April 1818, and besieged the Saudi capital. Supported by many local Bedouin tribes, who had grown weary of the exactions of the Saudis, the Egyptian forces surrounding Diriyah could count on secure lines of communication. Unlike the Saudis, who relied on light cavalry armed with traditional weapons, Ibrahim's Egyptian-led army was a semimodern force, with artillery, firearms, and professional leadership.

1818–1891

After an eight-month siege, on September 11, 1818, the Egyptians took Diri-yah and imprisoned Abdullah, who was eventually beheaded in Istanbul. The Egyptians and their Bedouin allies pillaged the Saudi capital, and razed its buildings in the hopes of forestalling a Saudi-Wahhabi renaissance. This final assault ended the first phase of the Saudi state in the Arabian Peninsula. That same year, the Egyptian/Ottoman force took Riyadh, and established treaties with local non-Saudi tribes to govern in the name of Muhammad Ali and the Ottoman Empire. Faced with sporadic resistance and attempts to revive the Saudi dynasty, the Egyptians resorted to massive retaliation against the civil-ian population of the Nejd, razing towns, executing prisoners, and imposing painfully heavy taxes. The Ottomans maintained garrisons in the principal cities of the Nejd—Riyadh, Shaqra, and Buraidah among them—but remained vulnerable to Bedouin attacks outside urban areas.

In Hijaz most of the population welcomed liberation from strict Wahhabi rule. Under Ottoman rule, the region brought back music, entertainment, and toleration for more liberal approaches to Islam. The Hijaz had long been host to religious minorities, including Shia and Sufi Muslims, who were once again able to practice their distinctive faith practices, as were Jews and Christians. The port of Jeddah, more than any other Arabian city, became host to hun-dreds of Europeans, Christian merchants, and travelers, who resided there to participate in the lucrative markets of the region. Even alcohol began to flow once again in the Hijaz, although Mecca and Medina did not immediately return to the wild days that preceded Saudi conquest. With the expulsion of the Wahhabis, trade returned, as did foreign visitors, and the pilgrimage to Mecca flourished, with Muslims rediscovering and restoring the holy sites of Islam after the years of ruin under the Saudis. Caravans from the three great Muslim cities—Cairo, Damascus, and Baghdad—once more brought tens of thousands of the faithful to the birthplaces of Islam, escorted by units of the Ottoman army. Although Istanbul appointed many of the sharifs, paid them subsidies from the Ottoman treasury, and maintained limited garrisons in Hijaz, these governors in practice had significant autonomy.

Although their dynasty had fallen, the Saudis retained the loyalty of most tribes in the Nejd, who continued to practice the Wahhabi sect. By the early 1820s, the Saudis had begun to reorganize and pose a threat to Egyptian/ Ottoman occupation of central Arabia. While Egyptian forces continued to dominate the peninsula, within a few years after the conquest of the Nejd they began to withdraw the bulk of their garrisons. While Ibrahim Pasha, Muham-mad Ali's son, was an effective general and governed the Nejd with strong, even cruel measures, the costs of the occupation were unsupportable. The same year as his great conquest, 1818, Ibrahim began to withdraw his forces to Hijaz. Before doing so, he took several hundred hostages from among the Saudi ruling class, leveled several key Saudi settlements, burned any trees and vegetation that had survived earlier assaults, and destroyed food stores and other goods that might be used by the dynasty.

Although Egyptian forces did not maintain any large garrisons in the Nejd, they continued to remain interested in the region. Subsequent governors of Arabia, appointed by Cairo, sent punitive expeditions into Nejd to preempt a Saudi resurgence, as well as any united front against the Ottomans. Careful to avoid confronting the British, who increasingly controlled the Persian Gulf, Egyptian military commanders were happy to allow central Arabia to remain ungovernable. For two decades after Ibrahmin's conquest of Diriyah, the Nejd remained a disunited, warring region, in which the Bedouin tribes returned to their traditional fighting, raiding, and shifting alliances. Egypt supported the efforts by Muhammad ibn Mishari ibn Muammar, a local emir, to increase his authority in the Nejd, but was content to allow his defeat in 1819. As the Saudis began to restore their strength, in 1820–1821, the Egyptians launched another attack in the Nejd, waging devastating attacks on villages and towns sympathetic to the Saudis. Once again unable to maintain a large occupation force, the Ottomans withdrew to the Hijaz, leaving small garrisons in Riyadh and other key cities.

In the Hasa, British campaigns against piracy were successful in the 1820s, and London established treaties with Oman, Bahrain, Kuwait, and other emirates along the Gulf Coast, transforming this zone into a clear sphere of influence. While not officially colonies or protectorates during these early stages, these states were coming increasingly under British control and protection, protection that would be tested greatly with the revival of Saudi fortunes and military strength in the coming decades.

In 1824, the new leader of the Saudi family, Turki ibn Abdullah ibn Muhammad ibn Saud, launched an attack on Riyadh, the center of Ottoman strength in the Nejd. Successful in this endeavor, Turki made Riyadh the new capital of the Saudi state, rather than returning to Diriyah, a city destroyed and plundered many times by the Ottomans and rival tribes. The occupation of Riyadh, and identification as the central city of the Saudis, began the second major phase of Saudi expansion. Refugees, driven away by the devastation of the Egyptian campaigns in the region, began to return. By the late 1820s, Turki had consolidated power in the Nejd, and turned east to the Hasa region along the Gulf Coast. Within a few years, he had gained authority over much of the region, exacting tribute from tribes along the coast. By 1830, the Saudis controlled most of the Hasa, even in zones that had never fallen under their authority previously. In 1834, Turki was assassinated while leaving Friday prayers, leading to several years of tumult and civil war. At the time of his death, the Saudi state had regained much of the territory it had lost to the Egyptians, controlling most of the peninsula outside of the Hijaz.

In 1831, Muhammad Ali declared his independence from the Ottoman Empire, and began a campaign to wrest Syria and southern Anatolia from Istanbul. Engaged against the Ottomans, Egypt's interest in Arabia continued to decline, as did its ability to influence events outside of the Hijaz. Even in that coastal region, sporadic rebellions against Egyptian rule, and rising enthusiasm for the Ottomans, forced Muhammad Ali to increase his garrisons. After Egypt and the Ottomans signed a truce, however, in 1837 Muhammad Ali launched another offensive into the Nejd, hoping to place a pliant Saudi, Khalid bin Sultan, in control of Riyadh. Initially the two sides fought to a standstill, and even contemplated a truce that would divide Arabia, but in 1838 Egypt and its Arabian allies attacked again.

In 1838, the Egyptians succeeded in placing Khalid ibn Saud, a son of the former ruler Saud, on the throne in Riyadh. By 1840, however, Egypt withdrew its forces from Arabia again, in what would become a permanent retreat. Weakened by opposition by the Western powers, as well as from the Ottomans, in 1840 Muhammad Ali had to accept the restoration of Ottoman sovereignty over Egypt. Britain, Russia, Austria, Prussia, and the Ottoman Empire had agreed that Egypt posed a threat to regional security, and imposed an ultimatum on Muhammad Ali: he must withdraw from occupied territories and submit to Ottoman rule again, or face international military action. The Europeans preferred the weak and decadent Ottoman Empire, in which they had significant investments and leverage, to a reformed, ambitious, and modernizing Egypt, which might resist the demands of the Great Powers. Although France had sponsored Muhammad Ali, they were unwilling to confront this powerful union of European powers, and advised the Egyptian to yield, which he did. Although he remained hereditary governor of Egypt, and retained autonomy within the Ottoman Empire, Muhammad's dream of creating a new Middle Eastern power died. Arabia, as a consequence, became officially part of the Ottoman Empire again, but only the Hijaz saw Turkish garrisons. Khalid, who had been put in power in large part through Egyptian intervention, became a close ally of the Ottomans.

In 1843, Faisal ibn Turki, taken prisoner in 1838, escaped from Egypt and returned to Nejd and declared himself Saudi emir. Gathering the old tribes and settlements together once again, he rallied his forces and retook Riyadh in 1843, overthrowing Khalid. He succeeded in retaking most of the original pre-1818 Saudi territory, excepting the Hijaz and the Hasa. Faisal strengthened the Saudi state and ruled until 1865, an uncharacteristically long reign in nineteenth-century Arabia. One of the greatest struggles of Faisal was over influence in the Persian Gulf, especially given rising British power in the region. As early as 1820, the British had occupied Bahrain, although this did not lead initially to a permanent base. In 1850, however, a Saudi attempt to force tribute from Bahrain met the guns of the Royal Navy. After several more years of jousting over the territory, in 1861 Bahrain became a British protectorate. Nonetheless, emir Faisal succeeded in consolidating control over central Arabia, resisting sporadic forays by sharifan forces. After the death of Faisal in 1865, however, his sons, Abdullah and Saud, fought a civil war for control over the Saudi state in the Nejd.

By the 1870s, Saudi control over the Nejd had declined precipitously, and they had lost the Hasa to the resurgent Ottomans. The Saudis still controlled Riyadh and had the loyalty of the ulama (religious teachers and imams), but infighting had weakened their ability to field warriors. The conflict between Abdullah and Saud drained Saudi resources, as the two brothers alternated in power. Both drew in outside support—Ottoman, British, and Rashidi—during their bitter rivalry, but neither was able to achieve a final victory. Torn by this civil war, the Saudi state continued to weaken. Additionally, the Shammar tribe, in alliance with the Rashidis, had gained influence and forged an alliance with the Ottomans. Talil al Rashid, the initial leader of the Shammar tribal confederation (1847–1868), allowed religious diversity within his territory, tolerating Shia Muslims, Jews, and Christians. Talil's eventual successor, Muhammad bin Rashid (1872–1897), began to expand from his base in Ha'il in the 1870s. Tribal affiliations and moderate policies ensured the initial success of the Rashidi state. Saudi fortunes were so low that even their capital, Riyadh, fell to the Rashidis in 1887, although a subsequent pro-Saudi uprising brought back the dynasty temporarily. In 1891, Rashid defeated the last army of the Saudis and occupied Riyadh. Abdul Rahman bin Faisal, the leader of the Saudi family, fled south to the desert wastes near the Rub al-Khali (Empty Quarter), protected by the Al-Murrah tribes, but under pressure from the Shammar's forces, he escaped through Bahrain to Kuwait.

1891–1902

With their second state crushed, the Saudi family escaped to Kuwait, where they found sanctuary with the emir, a long-standing enemy of the Rashidis and Ottomans. The former emir of Riyadh, Abd al-Rahman ibn Faisal Al Saud, took refuge there to plot his return to power. His eldest son, Abd al-Aziz ibn Abd al-Raghman ibn Faisal Al Saud, who would become the first king of Saudi Arabia, grew up in Kuwait, planning with his father for their eventual return to Riyadh. The alliance between the Saudis and the Kuwaitis continued, as internal conflicts in the Nejd continued throughout the 1890s. Protected by Britain, with whom it had long-standing security agreements, Kuwait felt free to intervene in the Arabian Peninsula, supporting the Saudis as the dynasty most likely to support its trade and familial interests. The

Rashidis formed an alliance with the Ottoman Empire, paying a nominal trib-ute and recognizing the Ottoman sultan as ruler, in exchange for weapons and diplomatic support. Thus strengthened, the Rashidis attempted to consolidate their control over the Nejd, although the perpetually unruly Bedouin tribes, as well as other traditional allies of the Saudis, prevented a final pacification of the region. The British, always interested in maintaining a balance of power in Arabia, began to provide clandestine support to the exiled Saudis, as well as encouraging Kuwait to continue its aid to the family. In 1899, with its ruler concerned about Ottoman ambitions, Kuwait became a formal protectorate of Great Britain, although this remained initially secret. Although the Otto-mans and British agreed in 1901 to avoid direct conflict with each other in the region, both continued to support their allies in Arabia, with the hopes of establishing a friendly regime.

While they had held central Arabia for decades, by 1900 the Rashidi-Shammar state was beginning to weaken. Although providing them with a powerful external ally, dependence on the Ottomans undermined the popu-larity of the Rashidis. Their rule was unpopular in non-Shammar areas, and unrest continued despite campaigns against rebellious provinces. The rise to power of Ibn Rashid, nephew of Muhammad, accelerated this decline. Favor-ing a strong hand to impose order, he raised taxes and plundered rebellious villages, gaining temporary victories but succeeding in increasing the breadth of resistance to his rule. With Ottoman encouragement and military aid, Ibn Rashid even launched an abortive attack on Kuwait in 1900, recognizing its role in encouraging pro-Saudi rebellion. He hoped through this action to annex Kuwait, an action the Ottomans believed would significantly weaken the British. Not only did his invasion fail, but it encouraged Kuwait to be more aggressive in its support of the Saudis, and also convinced the British of the need for action. Another invasion in 1901 achieved temporary gains at the expense of Kuwait, and Ibn Rashid massacred civilian populations in several communities. Angered at these brutal assaults on a client state, the British prevailed successfully on the Ottomans to stop supporting the Rashidis, and stationed a battleship and other ships in Kuwait's waters to repel future assaults.

In 1901, Ibn Saud left Kuwait with a handful of warriors to take the fight to the Rashidis. Gaining Bedouin allies along the way, he seized Riyadh with a small force of a few dozen, and sent word to Kuwait for his father to return to the city from exile. The population of the city and the surrounding tribal areas received the ruler of the revived Saudi dynasty, Abdul Aziz, as a hero. Abdul Aziz, however, immediately abdicated in favor of his son, Ibn Saud, who had led the military campaign to retake their homeland and earned tremendous popularity for his courage and audacity. Riyadh was once more the capital of a Saudi emirate.

Despite this bold victory, the restored Saudi state was weak. Many of the tribes and settlements in the Nejd remained allied to the Rashidis, suspicious of a Saudi-Wahhabi renaissance, or at best indifferent to the ruling dynasty in Riyadh. The Saudis and Rashidis fought several more battles, in late 1902 and early 1903, but the Saudis emerged victorious in each encounter. Over the next four years, Ibn Saud had to struggle to consolidate his control over the Nejd and western areas of the Hasa, establishing a permanent base for a state that would eventually control the entire Arabian Peninsula.

In addition to the British protectorates in the Persian Gulf, the Hijaz remained outside of Saudi authority during this period. The Ottoman Empire, after briefly losing control to the Egyptians in the 1830s, regained these provinces, and increasingly integrated them into their state. Deriving significant religious legitimacy from their role as the protectors and custodians of the holy cities of Mecca and Medina, sultans in the late nineteenth and early twentieth centuries strengthened and deepened their occupation. Not only did the Turks reassert control over the pilgrimages, they began to impose taxes on these visits, as well as on desert caravans and goods passing through the port of Jeddah. In 1900, the Ottomans revived a long-dormant plan to build a railway from Mecca to Damascus. Although construction did not begin until 1904, it would become an essential communications line, increasing trade and pilgrimages in the Hijaz, and enabling the Ottomans to maneuver their military units in the region much more rapidly.

The Saudi dynasty rose to power over the course of two centuries. Its progression, however, was far from steady, and at several points seemed on the verge of extinction at the hands of the Ottoman Empire. Egyptian, Turkish, and British forces, not to mention important Arab tribes, fought against Saudi military power and Wahhabi religious doctrine with fierce determination. The Saudi victory in 1902, however, began the final phases in what would become, in the twentieth century, the Kingdom of Saudi Arabia, an entity that would survive the collapse of the Ottoman and British Empires.

6

The Creation of Saudi Arabia (1902–1932)

With the recapture of Riyadh in 1902, the House of Saud was once again in control of its historical capital in Arabia, and dominated the central region of the peninsula. However, the Saudis were not the unchallenged masters of the Nejd and Hasa. The Ottoman Empire continued to control the eastern and western coasts through Arab allies, the British had a sphere of influence and a string of protectorates in the Persian Gulf, and other local rulers, especially the Hashemite dynasty in Mecca, had ambitions to increase their authority over all of Arabia. Despite these challenges, over the following 30 years, the Saudis defeated their enemies in the peninsula, maintained internal order, established a new kingdom, and survived the fall of the Ottoman Empire in the Middle East—a state that had been a powerful presence in the region since the fifteenth century. The remarkable story of the creation of the Kingdom of Saudi Arabia, a struggle that involved international diplomacy, military campaigns, and religious conflicts, is the focus of this chapter.

OTTOMAN CAMPAIGNS AGAINST THE NEW SAUDI STATE (1902–1906)

The victory of the Saudis in 1902 that revived their state in Riyadh did not end warfare in the Nejd. The Ottomans, now apprised of the threat, attempted to destroy the dynasty. In May 1904, the Ottomans authorized the Al-Rashidis, their traditional ally in the Nejd, to launch a punitive expedition against Riyadh. Ibn Rashid, hoping to regain his authority in Arabia, had invited the Turks to enter the province. From their base in Baghdad, the Ottomans dispatched eight battalions of infantry—perhaps as many as 4,500 regular Turkish soldiers to support the Rashidis in the campaign to defeat the Saudis, although for logistical and political reasons not all of these could be used simultaneously against the Saudis.

In the summer of 1904, 2,000 Arab and Turkish soldiers marched against the Saudis, but poor leadership, lack of material preparation, and the difficulties of waging warfare during the Arabian summer quickly dissipated this force, leaving only 500 effectives by October. Although the Turks were tough and disciplined soldiers, most of them were not acclimated to the harsh desert climate of Arabia, and suffered from food shortages, disease, and desertion. The Turkish forces also did not trust their Arab allies, believing with some justification that the Rashidis would break with them once the Saudi threat had faded. After the failure of their first effort, the Ottomans launched a renewed offensive in 1905, with forces from Basra, but a simultaneous rebellion in Yemen diverted greater potential reinforcements for the Rashidis in central Arabia, leaving the Saudis free to consolidate their control over the region. The April 1906 battlefield death of Ibn Rashid ended the last serious threat to Saudi control over central Arabia, although sporadic raiding continued from discontented tribes, such as the Shammar, that had been loyal to the Rashidis.

Conflicts with their local allies, logistical difficulties, and professions of loyalty by the Saudis led to a negotiated settlement in 1906; the Ottomans withdrew from the Nejd to the eastern Hasa and the western Hijaz, in exchange for nominal Saudi subordination, although this agreement survived only until the last Turkish soldiers withdrew from the Nejd. Of the more than four thousand Turks that had entered Arabia, perhaps only a thousand returned to Ottoman bases in Iraq and the Hijaz. Fresh from this strategic victory, but nonetheless vulnerable to an Ottoman change of heart, Ibn Saud repeatedly asked for security guarantees from the British. Unwilling to cause additional conflicts with the Ottomans, the British refused, forcing the Saudi ruler to hesitate before causing difficulties in Ottoman territory in eastern and western Arabia. Although in 1910 the British dispatched an army officer, Captain J. D. Shakespear, to advise Ibn Saud, they were unwilling to provide arms or encouragement to the Saudis at that time.

Saudi control over the Nejd, consolidate by 1908, was not without its challenges. A serious drought hit the region in 1908, and lasted three years, threatening the fragile oases and wells that made possible subsistence agriculture in the desert. Some Arabs believed that this lack of rain, which hit central Arabia while sparing the coasts, was a sign of Allah's displeasure at Saudi ascendancy, a belief that encouraged rebelliousness among the Bedouin tribes. Adding to the suspicion that there was a supernatural reason for the drought was the rainfall in the Rashidi territory of Jabal Shammar, outside the control of Ibn Saud. The imposition of the Wahhabi version of strict Sunni Islam, with its prohibitions of alcohol and tobacco (a ban later rescinded), limitations on traditional religious practices, and restrictions on women, were also not received well by Bedouin tribes accustomed to autonomy. The Rashidis, Turks, and others also continued to supply arms and grievances to resisting tribes, testing Saudi resolve and resources throughout the kingdom.

Although Ibn Saud had achieved a victory in the Nejd by 1906, it was a limited one, with serious economic and geographic challenges limiting the strength of the country. With no natural resources—major oil discoveries were decades away—and a heavy reliance on imports, the Saudi state ran a perpetual trade deficit. Ibn Saud's diplomatic and military skills had yielded him a kingdom, but it was one of the most isolated and poor on the planet. To his east, west, and north was the Ottoman Empire, which controlled access to the sea and boasted a modern army, European allies, and the potential to crush the small Saudi state. To the south was the vast Empty Quarter, which marked the ill-defined boundary with Ottoman Yemen and British-controlled Aden and Oman. Beyond the thin line of Ottoman control in eastern and western Arabia was the much more powerful British Empire, which from its bases in India, the Persian Gulf, and Egypt further constrained the Arabia Peninsula. To make the position of his kingdom tenable, Ibn Saud had to continue his expansion, without provoking the wrath of Istanbul or London: no small task.

SHARIF HUSSEIN AND THE HIJAZ (1908–1914)

Sharif Hussein, appointed by the Turks in 1908 as emir, was a vassal of Istanbul, having lived in the Ottoman capital before receiving his position. Raised among Bedouins before being sent to Istanbul, he had strong tribal links to the Hijaz and even stronger ambitions. Although formally a dependency of the Ottoman Empire, Hussein hoped to become increasingly important, asserting claims over the Nejd and other areas of the Arabian Peninsula. This vision matched Ottoman ambitions, and Turkish officials periodically urged the Arab ruler to launch forays into central Arabia to crush the Saudi upstarts. With limited indigenous means, few Turkish soldiers in the Hijaz, and the difficulties of fighting in the deserts of the Nejd, Hussein initially confined himself to periodic raids against tribes allied with the Saudis, who reciprocated with attacks on coastal territories.

During the first two years of his rule, Hussein had aided the Ottomans in the suppression of a major rebellion in Asir, highlands between the southern Hijaz and Yemen. After suppressing this uprising, which coincided with one against the Ottomans in Yemen, Hussein was free to turn more of his attention against Saudis. In 1910, Hussein led an invasion of the western reaches of the Nejd, capturing Saad, Ibn Saud's brother. Although the sharifan army was too small to conquer the Hijaz, he was able to force Ibn Saud into a humiliating truce. In exchange for the return of his brother, the Saudi ruler agreed to pay an annual tribute to Sharif Hussein and to accept nominal Ottoman sovereignty of the Nejd. After securing his brother's release, however, Ibn Saud failed to fulfill his commitments, but it seems unlikely that Hussein had ever expected compliance. The temporary humiliation of Ibn Saud was a limited victory, but given the modest means of the sharif, it was nonetheless a triumph.

In 1911, Asir again rose in revolt, and received assistance from Ibn Saud in their rebellion against the Ottomans and Sharif Hussein. Ottoman emissaries attempted to gain the loyalty of the Saudis, but Ibn Saud's suggestion that the Turks should sponsor a gathering of prominent Arabs, and offer them the opportunity to remain as separate vassals or unite in a single political entity, was not encouraging. Although the Saudis continued to profess their formal subordination to the Ottoman sultan, they did not pay taxes, allow Ottoman soldiers, merchants, or officials into their domain, nor support Turkish military operations in the Arabian Peninsula. Independent in everything but name, the Saudis aimed to hold off a major Ottoman assault, while at the same time taking advantage of weaknesses in the empire to increase the size of their own state in Arabia.

Relations between the Saudis and Sharif Hussein continued to be hostile, with events in 1912 adding to this antipathy. Hussein launched additional raids into the Nejd, leading his soldiers on attacks into pro-Saudi areas. Hussein also banned Nejdis from participating in the annual pilgrimage to the Holy Cities of Mecca and Medina. To the Wahhabis of the Saudi emirate, this was a bitter blow against their ability to fulfill one of the pillars of Islam. The prohibition also had a devastating impact on the economy of the Nejd, which had benefited from trade with the thousands of pilgrims who traveled through their region on their way to the Hijaz, or who purchased goods from their itinerant traders who operated along caravan routes during the hajj.

THE STRUGGLE FOR HASA (1906–1913)

Fortunately for Ibn Saud, the Ottomans, with their resources stretched thin across southeastern Europe, Anatolia, and the Middle East, paid little attention to Arabia in the early twentieth century, and even less to Hasa. By the late 1800s, the stability and security of the region had declined, as the limited policing provided by Ottoman garrisons was insufficient to deter Bedouin raids on settlements and towns. Arbitrary decisions by Ottoman governors in the allocation of water rights, the imposition of customs duties, and other issues decreased support for Istanbul, even if it did not cause local sheikhs to transfer their loyalty to the British or Saudis. The failure of the Turks to preserve and extend infrastructure into the region, such as rail lines, telegraph, or better roads, mitigated their ability to control Hasa or improve their reputation within the Arab population.

Ottoman military forces in the Hasa were never particularly strong. Despite the great expanse of the territory, for example, the Turkish units stationed in the region were nearly all infantry, in contrast to the mounted Bedouins they faced, who rode horses and camels. Mistrusting the loyalties of the local Arabs, the Turks also were reluctant to organize, arm, and train indigenous tribal units, despite the potential for gaining local assistance on security issues. The Turks did little to fight corruption, and in most cases were the causes and beneficiaries of bribes. Ill-conceived measures to fight the Saudi menace in the Nejd—such as imposing an embargo on trade from Hasa—did little to hurt the Saudis, but destroyed the livelihoods of some merchants in their own region. Ottoman tax increases in the decade preceding World War I contributed to resentment among the local population against what would be seen increasingly as a foreign occupation. The limited economy of the eastern peninsular Arabs depended on trade, especially on the pearl industry. From the ancient period forward, divers exploited the rich undersea terrain to harvest pearls for domestic use and export. It was only in the twentieth century that cultured pearls began to replace those recovered through saltwater pearl diving in the Indian Ocean and Persian Gulf, including off the eastern coast of Arabia.

Poor relations between the Turks and local Arabs would become significant with the final Saudi assault into Hasa in 1913. Although Ibn Saud had been reluctant to confront the Ottomans directly after his truce with them in 1906, he had over the years surreptitiously supported raids into the Hasa and encouraged turmoil in the region, attempting to create conditions favorable to his conquest. By 1912–1913, Istanbul was focused in the Balkan Wars, a potential rebellion in the Hijaz, and rising tensions with Russia and Austria. Taking advantage of the weakening Turkish position, Saudi forces seized the Hasa in 1913. After decades of neglect by the Ottomans, Hasa tribal leaders did not take sides, thus allowing the defeat of the Turkish garrisons. After some brief skirmishes, the Saudi forces allowed the Ottomans to evacuate the province. Following repeated reductions in the force because of other conflicts, by this time there were fewer than 500 Turkish soldiers in Hasa, clustered in small and immobile Ottoman garrisons that were continuing to decline as a result of disease and desertion. In May 1914, the Saudis and Ottomans concluded a treaty that accepted Saudi control of the region, but preserved nominal Ottoman sovereignty, including over foreign affairs. However, neither side implemented this agreement in good faith, and World War I left the treaty a dead letter.

Even with the annexation of the Eastern Province, Saudi power in eastern Arabia remained limited by the ongoing British presence: Kuwait, Bahrain, Qatar, Oman, and the Trucial States (later the United Arab Emirates) continued under the protection of the United Kingdom, connected to the British Empire by treaties of trade and military basing. With ties to the Crown Colony of India, these small Persian Gulf states could rely on military and political defense with London, effectively maintaining their autonomy from an expanding Saudi Arabia. A far greater threat to Saudi rule in Arabia was internal, however, emanating from one of the tools that had made the creation of the kingdom possible: the Ikwhan brotherhood. Although initially a tool of the nascent state, the brotherhood had begun to chafe against the modernizing intentions of the king. Before this threat became critical, however, Ibn Saud had to navigate his rising nation through the difficulties of a major global conflict, which would transform Europe, the Arab World, and the status of Islam: World War I.

WORLD WAR I IN ARABIA (1914–1918)

The Arabian Peninsula was not a major theater of war, but it did play an important secondary role, primarily as the scene of a British-supported Arab revolt against the Ottoman Empire. Although the Ottomans claimed most of Arabia, the fighting focused on the Hijaz, important to the Arabs and the Turks because of the Holy Cities of Mecca and Medina. The Hijaz was also critical because of its importance as a communications juncture, with access to the Red Sea, the railway that connected Damascus to Yemen, and the key port of Jeddah. The railway, finished in 1908, shortened overland travel time between Damascus and Medina from 40 days to 5. The 900-mile line, partially funded by donations from devout Muslims, not only eased travel for pilgrims, but also enabled Ottoman forces to move quickly to reinforce their besieged garrisons in time of war or domestic disorder.

With the Ottoman entry into World War I in October 1914 on the side of the Central Powers (Germany, Austria-Hungary, and Bulgaria), the Arabian Peninsula became a theater of war, albeit a minor one. The sharif of Mecca, Hussein ibn Ali, after being assured of British support, declared an Arab Revolt, seized Mecca, and declared himself king of the Arabs in 1916. Hoping to capitalize on rising Arab nationalism, Hussein encouraged Arab tribes and cities to rally to his cause and fight against the Turks. This revolt, led by his son Faisal, under the advice of the famous British officer T. E. Lawrence (Lawrence of Arabia), raided Turkish garrisons, took control of most of the Hijaz and, most notably, seized the strategic city of Damascus from the Ottoman Empire in October 1918.

Sharif Hussein, despite his ambitions, had supported the Turkish government in Istanbul, serving as their mostly loyal vassal and ensuring access to the Holy Cities for Ottoman pilgrims. The coming of a major European war, however, convinced him that the Ottomans were in decline. Campaigning under the banner of Arab unity, and by implication the idea of creating a single Arab state, Hussein and Faisal never concluded a formal agreement with the British that stated shared postwar aims. Although only a minor contributor to the overall campaign against the Central Powers, the Arab Revolt did become significant as the first serious expression of Arab national identity, albeit a frustrated one.

The Saudis did not participate in the revolt, expressing their discontent not that the movement pitted Muslims against Muslims, but that Hussein received subsidies, military aid, and guidance from a foreign Christian power in its war against the Ottomans. Even more important was the antipathy between Sharif Hussein and Ibn Saud. The Meccan leader at various times referred to the Saudi emir as "the son of a dog" and "intoxicated," both strong insults to any Arab, but especially a Wahhabi. Although Ibn Saud launched a few minor attacks on Ottoman outposts, he did not fully engage in the war. The most important diplomatic victory of Ibn Saud during World War I was the Anglo-Saudi Treaty of 1915, which recognized Hasa and the Nejd as Saudi territory in perpetuity, but also included Saudi acceptance of British protectorates over the Gulf States. The British also provided Ibn Saud with modest military and financial assistance to enable him to consolidate his rule over central and eastern Arabia, and forestall any potential Ottoman or Rashidi resurgence.

SAUDI CONQUEST OF THE HIJAZ

World War I ended with many issues unresolved among the Arabs. The dream of Sharif Hussein—to unite the Arabs into one great nation—remained frustrated by the imperial designs of the British and French, who preferred to create many weak Arab states rather than one potentially strong one. British and French interests in the Middle East became the defining measures in the region, subsuming local authorities and movements under the global power of these two European powers. The Sykes-Picot agreement of 1916 between France and the United Kingdom divided the Arab world between the two powers, with little attention to local desires. Even as the French asserted themselves in Lebanon, Syria, and northwest Africa, and the British in Palestine, Egypt, Iraq, and the Persian Gulf, the two states became decreasingly interested in central and western Arabia. Faisal, who had led the Arab Revolt during World War I, became king of Iraq, while his brother

Abdullah became Transjordan's monarch. Hussein remained King of the Hijaz, but claimed authority over all Arabs.

The close ties between the British and Sharif Hussein—exemplified by the experience of Lawrence of Arabia—did not long survive the end of World War I. By the early 1920s, Hussein had become frustrated with the failure of the British to support his greater ambitions, and his dream of uniting all Arabs under his rule. Hoping to increase his legitimacy and claims to broader powers, in 1924 he declared himself caliph, assuming the title after its abolition by the secularizing efforts of the Turkish Republic. This move provided Ibn Saud with the necessary pretext—heresy—to move against the Hijaz. In 1924, Ikhwan forces seized Mecca, in the process looting and killing several hundred of the town's residents, and imposing harsh punishments for those who violated strict Sharia, including bans on alcohol, music, and representative art. Although this was a tremendous military victory for the Saudi dynasty, the ferocity of the attack and the destruction that followed had a negative impact on the image of Ibn Saud among non-Wahhabi Muslims, and set the stage for a future conflict between the Saudi king and the Ikhwan.

By the end of 1925, Saudi forces had conquered the region, ousting the last Hashemite sharif and taking control over the ever-important holy cities of Mecca and Medina. Hoping to minimize some of the bad feelings engendered by the looting of the Holy Cities, Ibn Saud committed to restoring tombs and other important sites, so long as these locations did not become focal points for what he regarded as idolatry or saint worship. Abandoned by his British sponsor and seeing his army disintegrate in the face of Saudi attacks, Sharif Hussein abdicated in favor of his son and went into exile, to encourage his people to rally in defense of a new king, but this did not have the expected stimulating effect. Ali took refuge in the Red Sea port city of Jeddah, and was immediately confronted with a siege. After several months of resistance from Jeddah, Sharif Ali surrendered to the Saudis in January 1926. Recognizing the new reality, the civic and religious leaders of Mecca hailed Ibn Saud in the Grand Mosque as their king, uniting the peninsula under the Saudi dynasty.

Ibn Saud recognized that the Hijaz was not Riyadh. Although he appointed Wahhabi imams to lead the principal mosques in Mecca and Medina, he also constituted a Consultative Council for the nation, naming Hijazis to the body and taking seriously their advice. He also moved Ikhwan units away from Mecca and Medina, after several clashes between the ultra-orthodox militia units and foreign pilgrims. The king also used other military units to defeat or capture local bandits and tribes who had been raiding merchant caravans and pilgrims; in the new Saudi state, these practices were no longer acceptable or tolerated.

THE IKHWAN MILITARY ORDER

The House of Saud did not have a professional army during the founding of their state. Dependent on Bedouins from their tribes and those in alliance, their striking power was unreliable, based as it was on the ability of the Saudi emirs to promise and provide greater opportunities for glory and plunder than were available elsewhere in the peninsula. Loyalties in the region, however, shifted as frequently as the drifting sands. Faced with the demands of ongoing warfare, and the unpredictability of some of his allied tribes, Ibn Saud decided to create a more permanent and reliable military force, which would combine personal loyalty to him with a disciplined approach to spreading Wahhabism throughout the Arabian Peninsula.

Created in 1912, the Ikwhan (Brotherhood), was a devout force whose purpose was to provide Ibn Saud with a disciplined and organized military. The emir granted the Ikhwan land, seed, tools, and other means to cultivate lands in their reserved settlements, and soon tens of thousands of Bedouins flocked to the banners of the new militia. This was not a conventional army, however, but was instead an organization of Bedouins focused on jihad. To promote stability within his realm, Ibn Saud banned traditional raiding, and instead encouraged those wanting to fight to join the Ikhwan. Instead of attacking nearby tribes, the Ikhwan were to fight only when directed against the enemies of the Saudi dynasty, embracing holy war (jihad) under the guidelines of Wahhabi religious doctrine. Settled in *hujar* (segregated Wahhabi communities), the Ikwhan were Ibn Saud's primary strike force, and numbered over 60,000 strong. Although Ibn Saudi continued to field units comprised of men from his own tribe as well as those of his allies, the Ikhwan provided the fanatical assault troops for his army.

The weapon created by Ibn Saud to wage a war of conquest in Arabia—the Ikhwan Brotherhood—proved difficult to adapt to the demands of a nation at peace. Holy warriors without a war, the fierce Bedouins of the brotherhood soon grew discontented with the end of the war in the mid-1920s, and even more so with what they saw as the new kingdom's accommodations to the West and surrounding states. Ibn Saud's relationship to the Bedouin tribes was often ambivalent—they supported him on the battlefield, but often caused him serious difficulties during lulls in warfare, as these periods diminished opportunities for glory and plunder. The Ikhwan was the Saudi king's main weapon to repress these revolts, over two dozen of which occurred between 1916 and 1930.

Fanatical in their faith, they rode into battle fearless and terrifying, welcoming death as their promised path to paradise. The Ikhwan also viewed themselves as a moral force within the Saudi state, tasked with enforcing strict

Wahhabi religious laws, punishing unorthodox behavior, and attacking those who refused to comply, even tribes allied with Ibn Saud. The warriors opposed the use of modern technology that had not been available during the lifetime of the Prophet Muhammad, and destroyed telephone lines, automobiles, and rail lines, despite decrees by religious leaders that most technology was acceptable since the Prophet did not explicitly prohibit it. Even more challenging to Ibn Saud, the Ikhwan advocated continuing the war to unite the Arabs beyond the traditional boundaries of Arabia. Ibn Saud realized that to do so would cause war with the British Empire, which by the mid-1920s controlled directly or as protectorates the Arab states that bordered Arabia: Iraq, Transjordan, Kuwait, Muscat and Oman, Qatar, the Trucial States (United Arab Emirates), and Aden (Yemen). In 1929, Ikwhan dissatisfaction led to open revolt, but by late 1930 Ibn Saud had crushed the uprising, thanks in large part to his embrace of modern weapons.

THE BEGINNINGS OF THE PETROLEUM INDUSTRY

The existence of Saudi Arabia owed its early existence to the suffrage of the British government, which had allowed the House of Saud to base itself for years in Kuwait. The withdrawal of British support from the Hashemites in Mecca also made possible the final Saudi conquest of the peninsula. Nonetheless, the Saudi kingdom did not want to become another protectorate, falling under the authority of the British Empire. Ibn Saud, realizing the vulnerability of his weak nation to more powerful Western nations, quickly embraced the opportunities provided by the discovery of oil in the 1920s to establish ties with another foreign power: the United States. Thus, from early in its existence, the Saudis saw a relationship with the United States, based on oil and security, as key to maintaining their independence.

Initial ties with the United States did not emerge from an interest in exploiting potential oil reserves, but rather from activities that were more mundane. In 1911, ten of Ibn Saud's soldiers, wounded in a local skirmish along the Persian Gulf, received treatment at an American hospital in Bahrain, a missionary facility of the Reformed Church. Touched by the Americans' compassion, and impressed by their skills, the Saudi ruler invited the mission to send expeditions to his kingdom, including treating him in 1923, when the king was suffering from facial cellulitis. Other American visitors, including Charles Crane, Woodrow Wilson's representative to the Middle East after World War I, convinced the king that Americans were more generous and trustworthy than the British—a conclusion he maintained for the remainder of his life.

In the early 1930s, Ibn Saud agreed to allow Crane and his associates to prospect for water and gold across the peninsula. Crane sent an engineer, Karl Twitchell, to Jeddah in 1931, primarily to search for artesian wells and other aquifers. On later trips, Twitchell also looked for evidence of valuable ores, especially gold, and made improvements to the municipal water system in Jeddah. Crane financed these expeditions, and in 1931–1932 agreed to support a general geological survey of Arabia, in hopes of discovering lucrative minerals as well as petroleum. Twitchell and Crane also contacted U.S. oil companies, hoping to secure financial support for exploration in exchange for oil concessions in the kingdom.

Although the Iraq Petroleum Company, a British firm that had more experience in the region, was also interested in a contract with Ibn Saud, the king's predisposition to deal with Americans was the deciding factor. By the end of 1932, Standard Oil of California (SoCal) agreed to send a negotiator to meet with Ibn Saud with the goal of signing an agreement to jointly explore and exploit potential petroleum finds. The U.S.-Saudi petroleum relationship had begun, although it had yet to yield any major financial rewards for either side. In future decades, these economic and strategic partnerships would be essential for the security of the Kingdom of Saudi Arabia and the United States.

THE KINGDOM OF SAUDI ARABIA: STRUCTURE AND POLITICS

With the military campaigns to conquer most of Arabia complete, Ibn Saud had before him the more complicated task of uniting the peninsula into one political state. The Saudi state imposed its Wahhabi Islam over the rest of the new nation, introducing its strict version of Sunni law into areas, such as the Hijaz, that had allowed more liberal interpretations. Among the practices banned were drinking, prostitution, Shia veneration of shrines, and toleration of religions other than Islam. These rules, and a new uniform system of laws based on Hanbali jurisprudence, gradually replaced local legal systems derived from Bedouin customs and traditions.

During the early 1920s, the Saudi "state" was quite rudimentary. With few roads, no telegraph or telephone lines, no civil service, and a mostly uneducated ruling class, Ibn Saud's direct authority often did not extend beyond the line of sight of his royal court. Over the course of the decade, however, the state began to take form, with basic offices to collect taxes, conduct foreign policy, and extend the reach of the government into the provinces. Politics had no formal existence, but was instead managed personally through the person of the king. Through his meetings with tribal leaders, foreign dignitaries, and ulama (religious scholars), Ibn Saud increasingly asserted his authority over his large and isolated kingdom.

Given the shortage of educated peninsular Arabs who conformed to Wahhabi doctrine, Ibn Saud demonstrated a willingness to employ Muslims from outside his territory in key positions. This decision also ensured that these officials would not have any preexisting loyalties to tribes other than the king. The king employed Arabs from Mosul, Palestine, Egypt, Syria, and Libya, in many cases keeping these key advisers at his side for decades. Having attracted their service when the Saudi state was poor and isolated, he could trust their faithfulness after it became flush with oil wealth in the decades that followed.

As an absolute monarchy, the king was at the center of all decisions, including choosing a new title for his state. On September 23, 1932, Ibn Saud declared the creation of the Kingdom of Saudi Arabia, taking the title King Abd al-Aziz. For the first time, Arabia would be identified as the property of one dynasty, the Saudis, whose family name became an adjective in the official title of the state. Although the new nation had finally united the peninsula, it faced a legion of challenges, including heavy debts, declining pilgrimages, and simmering resistance to the Saudi dynasty, especially in the west and south.

FOREIGN RELATIONS OF THE SAUDI STATE

From the mid-nineteenth century until World War I, the two most important powers in the Middle East were the Ottoman Empire and the United Kingdom. As a result, the initial decades of Saudi foreign policy focused on preventing these two states from coordinating an assault on the rising dynasty. During the early decades of the twentieth century, Ibn Saud hoped to gain recognition, military aid, and economic benefits from cultivating a relationship with the United Kingdom. His ties with the Ottomans were more difficult, with long periods of hostility alternating with negotiated ambivalence. Although the Saudis confronted Ottoman garrisons and Arab proxies in eastern and western Arabia, Ibn Saud seldom fought Turkish troops directly, and on several occasions negotiated truces with Istanbul.

British uncertainty about the Saudis began with contacts in the early twentieth century. While the United Kingdom had no desire to conquer the arid and resource-poor territory, they did want to ensure the security of their Gulf protectorates against potential threats. British commercial interests in the Ottoman Empire before World War I also discouraged the empire from allowing confrontations with the Turks. During World War I, however, the British supported Arab resistance to Ottoman occupation and lent modest support to the Saudis. The end of that war, the collapse of the Ottoman Empire, and the subsequent Saudi conquest of the peninsula by the mid-1920s transformed the region in significant ways.

By the late 1920s, foreign states that had been more familiar with the Sharifan state and the Ottoman Empire accepted the new reality of Saudi Arabia. Having worked with Ibn Saud unofficially for years, the British extended formal recognition in 1927, in exchange for Ibn Saud's promises to respect Britain's protectorates in the Persian Gulf and safeguard British subjects on pilgrimage to Mecca, although tensions remained over the British mandates over Arab Palestine and Iraq. Other major European states also extended formal diplomatic ties at the same time, including the Soviet Union (1926), France (1926), and Germany (1929). Because of the isolation of Riyadh, the support among Wahhabi religious leaders and the dynastic court for keeping foreigners out of the traditional Saudi court, and the desire by foreign emissaries to maintain contact with their home countries, these initial diplomatic legations operated from Jeddah, only occasionally allowed to make the long trek to the capital of Riyadh.

The Red Sea port, which boasted not only a relatively modern harbor with routes to Egypt and India, but also wireless and telegraph connections beyond Arabia, had long been the most cosmopolitan city in the Hijaz, and host to the Ottoman garrisons until their expulsion in World War I. Ties to the Soviet Union were especially tenuous. Even though the two states negotiated the possibility of a more developed financial and trade relationship in the early 1930s, with Soviet leader Joseph Stalin offering treaties of friendship and commerce, the divide between the two states proved too great and the arrangement collapsed. In 1938, Karim Khakimov, the Soviet ambassador to Saudi Arabia, was recalled to Moscow, and disappeared in Stalin's purges. The Saudis instead depended on their long-standing relationship with Britain, and on rising commercial links to other Western states.

Perhaps indicating their hesitations about the fierce Islam of the new state, many Muslim states, including Persia and Egypt, did not recognize the Saudi state until the 1930s. The long decades of moderate Ottoman rule, as well as the suspicion that the upstart dynasty from Riyadh would be short-lived, caused some hesitation. More importantly, Saudi destruction of tombs and shrines in the Hijaz was a major factor in stoking conflict with Muslims from other nations, as were the Saudi restrictions on pilgrimages during the 1920s and 1930s. In the event, the arrival of the Great Depression after 1929 limited the numbers of Muslims who could afford the significant expense of the hajj.

Even so, after the initial destruction of many important religious sites in Mecca and Medina by the Ikhwan, Ibn Saud attempted to improve his image in the Islamic world. Among his efforts to aid pilgrims, he allowed automobiles on the pilgrimage route for the first time in history, kept pilgrims' fees low, and convened an international conference on the future of the Hijaz in 1926. Ibn Saud's efforts to improve the security yielded significant results, with reports of Bedouin attacks and petty crime declining significantly in the late 1920s. With bans on prostitution, alcohol, and even tobacco altering the social landscape of the Hijaz, however, many less devout Muslims, who had viewed the hajj as more of a vacation than a time of religious purity, stayed away from the region.

ECONOMY OF THE KINGDOM

Arabia in the late 1920s and early 1930s was one of the least developed regions in the world. With almost no arable land or exportable products, it also had one of the most illiterate populations in the Middle East. At the time of Ibn Saud's conquest of the Hijaz in the mid-1920s, it had no functioning railroads, telegraphs, telephones, paved roads, airfields, universities, factories, power plants, refineries, trade schools, or other elements of a modern infrastructure. The primary means of external revenue was the hajj—fees and other spending by thousands of pilgrims who made the annual trek to Mecca and Medina, in fulfillment of one of the pillars of Islam. However, Wahhabi restrictions on this practice, as well as the global depression of the 1930s, severely limited income from this activity.

The Saudi state thus stumbled along from one financial crisis to another during its first decade. Merchants who extended credit often received token payments for their efforts, and even long-term employees of the king had to wait six to eight months for their salaries. On several occasions, Ibn Saud had to temporarily default on loan payments to domestic and foreign creditors, as his fiscal difficulties continued unabated. Despite this ongoing poverty, the king undertook several measures to improve conditions and his authority, including establishing a national wireless radio network and building roads in the Hijaz to aid pilgrims in their journeys to the Holy Cities. His own spending on his entourage, visitors, and petitioners to his court, however, was one of the biggest expenses. Although King Abd al Aziz did not himself indulge in luxurious living, he tolerated it among other members of the ruling family, saddened as he often was by demonstrations of conspicuous consumption.

The king's treasurer, Abdullah Suleiman, who had learned some bookkeeping in India, attempted to introduce some limits on spending, especially for the royal family, but these efforts met with limited success. The king himself refused to accept limitations on his own munificence, and regarded unspent funds in the treasury as a mandate to give more generously. The kingdom did not have any financial reserves, overseas investments, or other monetary assets, living instead from monthly revenues, or dependent on periodic loans when state income came in lower than expectations and spending.

Poor, isolated, and constrained by an undeveloped infrastructure and mostly uneducated population, the weak economy of Saudi Arabia did not offer much hope in the early 1930s. Still plagued by bitter conflicts between its major tribes and a weak central administrative authority, it was a nation-state in little more than a nominal fashion. Emerging as an independent and internationally recognized state in the depths of global depression, the kingdom's fiscal and political future did not look promising. However, in the years that followed, the exploitation of its most precious natural resource—petroleum—would transform Saudi Arabia into a state with international importance, high standards of living, and close economic and strategic ties to the West, especially the United States.

7

The Kingdom of Ibn Saud (1932–1973)

An Arab tribesman who somehow managed to travel from 1632, 1732, or 1832 to witness the founding of the Kingdom of Saudi Arabia in 1932 would feel almost entirely at home. His way of life, culture, and tribal system did not change in many significant ways, even with the overlay of a unified political system under the Saudi dynasty. Even after the political consolidation of Ibn Saud's state in the 1920s, modernity and technology initially made only the most superficial appearance. Outside of a handful of modest-sized cities, Arabia remained as it had been for centuries: desert crisscrossed by nomadic tribes, with little economic activity. Beginning in the 1930s, however, and continuing for the next four decades, Saudi Arabia transformed, to the point that the Bedouin from a previous century would have felt hopelessly lost.

Sprawling metropolises, advanced infrastructure, heavy industry, and a demographic revolution arose rapidly in the years that followed the creation of the kingdom. It was during this period that Saudi Arabia developed from an essentially medieval tribal society into a modern state, driven by the centralizing effort of government, external influences, and the flush of massive revenues from the nation's most important resource: petroleum. While the kingdom still boasted of its camels, tribal ancestry, and Bedouin ways, the truth was that these had become increasingly vestigial, in a modern Saudi Arabia that struggled to adapt its culture and values, not always successfully, to the demands of a modern technological society. An absolute monarchy in a region increasingly governed by radical or authoritarian secular regimes, Saudi Arabia's system nonetheless survived, despite the hostility of the more powerful states in the Middle East, including Egypt, Iran, Iraq, and Israel. A strong relationship with the United States, fortunate geography, and skilled international maneuvering preserved the Saudi monarchy through these difficult decades, but not without significant challenges, both internal and external.

SAUDI ARABIA IN THE GREAT DEPRESSION

Saudi Arabia was poor at the beginning of the Great Depression, as it was at the end. For the Saudi dynasty, the period was typical of its history of poverty, but also saw the stirrings of the potential for riches, as the first major oil concessions revealed vast deposits of petroleum under the rock and sand of the Arabian Peninsula. The global economic crisis, however, depressed demand for oil and limited foreign capital available for exploration and exploitation of this resource. The stability of the regime was tested by this decade, but those that followed added immeasurably to the economic and political strength of the state. Over time, the major domestic social classes—Bedouins, merchants, religious leaders, and settled farmers—saw their interests aligned with the Saudi state, despite the diminished local autonomy that accompanied the rising central power of Riyadh. Three new classes—industrial workers, Western technical specialists, and rising numbers of foreign laborers—had more challenging relationships with the Saudi monarchy during later decades.

Despite Ibn Saud's consolidation of internal power, relations with the surrounding states were not always warm. In 1932, for example, the Saudis discovered a plot by exiles from the Hijaz, based in Yemen, to overthrow the Saudi king. Yemeni forces invaded the Asir region of southwestern Arabia in 1933, supported by arms sales and diplomatic aid from the Italians and British. In early 1934, the Saudi military counterattacked, drove the Yemenis and their Hijazi allies out of Saudi Arabia, and occupied several towns in Yemen. Under strong pressure from the Italians, French, and British, including the presence of European warships near Saudi territorial waters, the two sides negotiated an armistice in May 1934, which restored the prewar boundaries and pledged noninterference in each other's internal affairs. Although the Saudis were forced to withdraw under foreign threat, their tactical success demonstrated that Abd al Aziz could rally his forces in defense of external threats, albeit a modest one from a smaller and weaker neighbor.

During the 1930s, the Saudi state began to create some of the institutions of a permanent regime, including a national budget (1934) and taxes (primarily the Islamic zakat, or tithe). The king did not create a formal civil service, state bureaucracy, diplomatic corps, or cabinet during this period, relying instead on informal advisers, tribal alliances, and wealthy Saudis (and a few foreigners). Ibn Saud also accelerated his practice of intermarriage, taking wives from every major tribe and region, although never more than four at one time, following Islamic law. By some estimates, he had married and divorced over 200 women, fathering almost 100 children in the process. He continued to provide financial support to the women he divorced, thus maintaining ties to their regions and tribes, and accepted most of the sons of these marriages into his royal court. These sons would comprise the ruling class of the kingdom, and would become the kings, many of the cabinet ministers, and other high officials of Saudi Arabia into the twenty-first century.

Although he unified the peninsula through his charisma, travels, and marriages, Ibn Saud did not establish many central institutions, preferring to maintain unity through personal loyalties to him, following the traditional tribal pattern. For example, under his reign Saudi Arabia did not create a unified military, perhaps fearing such an institution might become a source of opposition, as had happened previously with the Ikhwan. Instead, the king created several armed forces and security units, allowing them to compete for arms, funding, and missions. This deliberate policy of allowing competition within the government added to the already significant challenges for the new state. Before oil became consistently profitable, the monarchy's greatest source of revenue, the pilgrimage to the holy cities of Mecca and Medina, remained vulnerable. During the 1930s, fees and other revenues associated with the hajj declined with the global depression. Over 100,000 pilgrims made the journey annually in the 1920s, but by the mid-1930s this number had fallen to 20,000. The state operated in continual national deficits, kept afloat by loans, modest revenues from pilgrimages and trade, and sporadic royalties from foreign companies prospecting for oil.

Saudi Arabia remained an absolute monarchy; none of the king's advisers, ministers, governors, or other officials developed independent authority. An example of this direct rule came in the form of the daily audiences, or majlis, held by the king. Any subject, whether a prince or poor Bedouin, could petition Abd al Aziz personally, asking for him to dispense justice or mercy in favor of the petitioner. No matter was too small for the majlis—resolving disputes over stolen goats or diverted water supplies, settling arguments over debts or land ownership, or assisting those made destitute through disasters or other tragedies. The king served as prosecutor, defense attorney, and judge all at once in these audiences, dispensing quick judgments on matters from the trivial to the most serious.

While this practice enabled the king to listen to his people, it also diverted him from more significant affairs of state, taking up as it did an inordinate amount his daily schedule. The king also maintained the traditional tribal practice of giving gifts to each petitioner, typically cloaks and daggers, but often money or presents of much greater value: expensive jewelry, handmade carpets, or even slaves. The expense to the state was a heavy burden, especially given that the king always provided food, lodging, and travel costs home after their visits, but the monarch refused to listen to advisers who suggested he should limit these audiences. Petitions also began to come to the king through other venues, including letters, telephone calls, and radio transmissions; Abd al Aziz insisted on hearing these requests as well, a daunting challenge given the rising population and developing communications infrastructure.

The king always had first call on state revenues, for gifts to his petitioners, grants to loyal tribal leaders, or imported goods that interested him. His finance minister, Abdullah al Suleiman, managed the kingdom's finances on a very simple level, fulfilling the king's demands, then making installment payments on the monarchy's foreign creditors, and then paying local contractors and salaries of government employees.

WORLD WAR II

During the decade preceding World War II, King Abd al Aziz played a minor role in Middle East politics, deferring on most issues to the leadership of Great Britain. Once war came to Europe in 1939, Saudi Arabia remained neutral. The king's sympathies were mostly with the Allies, despite some unhappiness with the British role in the Middle East. He saw fascism as a form of state and leader worship, at odds with his vision of his own conservative and monarchist government, which he believed needed to be subordinated to divine law and made to abide by tradition. Still, he understood the sympathy many Arabs felt for the revisionism of the Axis, and the identification of many Muslims in the Middle East with the anti-Jewish efforts of the Nazis. Adding to this ambivalence was Ibn Saud's hostility to atheistic communism, which prevented a rapprochement with Stalin's Soviet Union, even had the communist dictator been interested. Counterbalancing this antipathy to the Union of Soviet Socialist Republics (USSR) was an increasingly warm relationship with the United States, which had begun in the 1930s as a result of growing American interest in finding new petroleum sources, and a Saudi lack of interest in overturning the international order.

Ties between the United States and Saudi Arabia came even closer during World War II, when the two countries worked closely to guarantee the security of oil production and sent high-level delegations to each other's nations.

The high point of the U.S.-Saudi relationship came in February of 1945, when President Franklin Roosevelt met with King Ibn Saud on the U.S. warship *Quincy* near the Suez Canal. Although they disagreed on the resettlement of Jews into Palestine, Ibn Saud agreed to declare war on the Axis, to allow the United States to build a temporary air base in Dhahran, and to allow U.S. Navy ships to use Saudi ports during the conflict. President Roosevelt also promised to consult with the Saudi king before making any unilateral moves to support an independent Jewish state in Palestine.

Although their meeting was brief, the two leaders developed an immediate bond, cemented by the American president's gestures of friendship, including pitching a tent on the deck of the navy ship. After the meeting, which marked the first time Abd al Aziz had left Saudi Arabia since becoming king, President Roosevelt sent as a gift an American DC-3 aircraft to the Saudi king, outfitted with a rotating throne that always faced Mecca, and accompanied by an American aircrew. The meeting upset Prime Minister Winston Churchill, who viewed the Middle East as within the British sphere of influence, but a rushed meeting with Ibn Saud was not as fruitful as the one with the American president.

Although Ibn Saud harbored warm feelings toward, and increasing commercial ties with, the United States, its primary focus was on diplomacy within its region. Saudi Arabia was a founding member of the Arab League, formed as the "Society of Arab States" in March 1945. This organization, which also included Egypt, Iraq, Syria, Transjordan, and Lebanon, had as its purpose to promote the prevention of outside domination of the region. King Ibn Saud was not especially interested in the actions of the league, especially its increasingly anti-British and anti-American campaigns. The most important issue during the early years of the league was that of Palestine: preventing a Jewish state from rising. Palestine, despite not having a state, was granted observer status in the organization. Upon Israel's declaration of independence, the Arab League declared against the Zionist state, but Saudi Arabia did not send forces against Israel in 1948, unlike other member states. Although concerned for the rights of Palestinians, Ibn Saud was not willing to risk his nation's future on behalf of his fellow Arabs. He was too dependent on American oil concessions, and had little interest in events beyond his borders.

PETROLEUM AND FOREIGN CONCESSIONS

Although initial exploration for oil in Saudi Arabia had begun in the 1920s, it was not until the early 1930s that these expeditions yielded tangible results. The American geologist Karl Twitchell, who surveyed Saudi Arabia in the early 1930s, identified terrain in the Eastern Province that harbored likely deposits of petroleum. The king had initially hoped Twitchell would find underground water aquifers, but upon hearing of the potential for oil, encouraged the search. Based on Twitchell's work, King Ibn Saud signed an agreement with Standard Oil of California (SoCal) in 1933, granting the American company oil concessions in exchange for cash and loans. By 1935, the Americans had discovered oil in the province and had begun drilling. By 1938, SoCal had begun commercial production in Saudi Arabia, and by 1939 was producing over 500,000 barrels annually.

The role of the Americans in the new Saudi industry was surprising. The Middle East, including the Arabian Peninsula and the Persian Gulf, had been dominated for decades by Britain, which had established protectorates or other dependent relationships with most states in the region. The British had signed agreements to gain oil concessions in Iraq, Kuwait, Bahrain, and elsewhere, and had been instrumental in aiding in the rise of the Saudi state during World War I. However, Ibn Saud did not want to become just another client state of the British, preferring a strictly economic arrangement with the Americans to a more comprehensive relationship with the world's leading colonial power. Moreover, the Saudi turn toward the United States paralleled rising resentment in the Arab world against long-standing British dominance of the region. One final factor was the American offer to pay for their concession in gold, a commodity that the king understood as universal, rather than in paper currency.

Beginning in 1933, American geologists and engineers began prospecting seriously in Saudi Arabia. After more than four years of searching, with little more than dry wells and a few new water sources for the kingdom, in March of 1938, the SoCal teams discovered oil near Dhahran. By early May 1939, the wells were commercially viable, and the first oil tanker, loaded with Saudi crude, cruised through the Persian Gulf. The beginning of World War II in September, however, disrupted this slowly developing industry.

By the end of World War II, Saudi oil production had risen to more than 20 million barrels annually. Although much of the wartime boom in production went directly to fuel Allied vehicles and aircraft, postwar oil extraction continued unabated as the world's economy recovered, led by the United States. Rising demand for oil, and the kingdom's desire to extract as much wealth as possible from its only exportable commodity, led to unforeseen problems. Aramco (the Arabian American Oil Company), which dominated Saudi oil fields, endured labor unrest among its workforce during the late 1940s. Initially, most workers hired by the oil company were Saudi subjects—over 15,000 by the early 1950s. Hoping to retain these scarce skilled workers, Aramco provided housing, health care, education, and other benefits to the laborers and their families, conditions unheard of for skilled or industrial workers elsewhere in the kingdom.

Given the shortages of workers in Saudi Arabia, however, Aramco had contracted hundreds of skilled and unskilled laborers from outside the kingdom, most of them foreign Arabs, but also South Asians and other nationalities. Although the Saudi government resisted efforts by these workers to unionize, Aramco acceded to some demands, including better pay and housing, shorter workweeks, an eight-hour day, and improvements in working conditions and safety rules. Despite these difficulties, Saudi oil production continued to rise throughout the 1940s and 1950s. Revenues to the monarch increased from $10 million to $50 million between 1946 and 1950, while overall daily production grew from approximately 150,000 barrels to over 500,000 during that same period. At least during the 1950s, Saudi workers constituted the largest group within Aramco, making up over two-thirds of the total employees by the end of the decade.

Ibn Saud saw the rising production and profits, and demanded a renegotiation of the concessionary agreements with Aramco. After some difficult discussions, the Saudis achieved a new arrangement, gaining 50 percent of the profits made by the company. In one year, 1950–1951, revenue to the Saudi government grew from $57 million to $110 million. Arabia was fundamentally unprepared for this flow of revenue, with an uneducated population, an underdeveloped state, and the king grower weaker as his health declined in the early 1950s. The challenge of managing an expanded educational system and literacy clashed with the monarchy's need to maintain tight social control; for example, in the late 1940s and early 1950s, state funds subsidized hundreds of Saudi students at Western universities, but it was these elite students, most of them scions of the extended royal family, who contributed most to demands for reforms and more rapid Westernization during the decades that followed.

Surprisingly little state revenue under Abd al Aziz went to infrastructure, health, education, or other services for his subjects. Aside from a few rail lines, roads, and radio transmission stations, which in any case represented nods to security as much as economic activity, the king did not spend his treasury on developing services. He preferred to share wealth personally and directly to individuals, rather than develop the broader economy. Royalties continued to increase over the next few years, flooding the monarchy with unprecedented cash. By 1960, over 80 percent of government revenue came from oil revenue, representing an economy almost entirely dependent on one source of income.

THE ARAB LEAGUE AND THE NEW MIDDLE EAST

The end of World War II forced the United Kingdom, weakened and indebted by the conflict, to reduce its global commitments dramatically. By the end of 1947, Britain had withdrawn its support for Greece, granted India and Pakistan independence, and abandoned Palestine. Into this void rushed the United States under President Truman, providing aid to Greece and Turkey, increasing political and military ties in the region, and supporting the establishment of the state of Israel in 1947–1948. This latter action was poorly received in Saudi Arabia, seen as a betrayal of the late President Franklin Roosevelt's promise to consult with King Abd al Aziz before taking any major action on the Jewish question. Truman, however, had not been privy to those discussions, and was more concerned with domestic politics than with Arab sensitivities over Palestine and Zionism.

In this environment, newly independent and assertive Arab governments united to make common cause against any effort to reassert foreign occupation or external control in the region. After more than 20 years of British bases, mandates, unequal treaties, trade favoritism, and influence from Egypt to Iraq, support for breaking with London was at an all-time high in the Arab world of the 1940s and 1950s. Anger over Britain's tolerance for Jewish emigration to Palestine, the Anglo-French-Israeli attack on Egypt in 1956, and the realization that the United Kingdom was gradually dismantling its empire, encouraged Arab states to establish new arrangements. The United States, and later the Soviet Union, would be the prime beneficiaries of this search for new great-power relationships. As a state without a reputation as an occupying power in the region, and eager to develop commercial relationships without political entanglements, the United States was, except for its support of Israel, an appropriate partner for Saudi Arabia and like-minded Arab states.

Saudi diplomatic ties with other Arab states were not always close. Relations were cool with Iraq, given Ibn Saud's employment of Rashid Ali—a pro-German former Prime Minister who had attempted to overthrow the Iraqi monarchy in 1941—and cross-border raids launched by tribes in both nations. Given the Hashemite backgrounds of the Iraqi and Transjordanian kings, it was no surprise that the House of Saud did not embrace warmly these ancestral enemies. Ibn Saud and his successors tried to maintain friendly ties with Egypt and Syria, but instability and regime changes in both made this an ongoing challenge. The military coup that overthrew Egypt's King Farouk in 1952 heralded the beginnings of almost two decades of tension between Cairo and Saudi Arabia, as the charismatic Egyptian officer Gamal Abdul Nasser became the revolutionary leader of the Arab masses.

SAUDI ARABIA AND THE BEGINNING OF THE COLD WAR

Saudi Arabia generally aligned with the United States during the Cold War, viewing the Soviet Union's official embrace of atheism as anathema to the teachings of Muhammad. Additionally, the Saudi oil industry was closely linked to markets in the West, especially the United States. While the warm ties forged between President Roosevelt and King Ibn Saud did not survive FDR's death in 1945, the two nations continued to work together. In 1951, the United States and Saudi Arabia signed a mutual defensive pact, committing the United States to assist Riyadh, and also allowing the United States to maintain an air base in Dhahran, first used during World War II. Tensions began to increase between the two nations in the mid-1950s, especially with U.S. encouragement of a British-led regional security alliance, the Baghdad Pact, among Iran, Iraq, Turkey, Pakistan, and the United Kingdom. While ostensibly anticommunist, the pact included Iraq and Iran, both of whom had difficult relations with Saudi Arabia. To counteract the Baghdad Pact, Saudi Arabia began to cooperate more with Egypt, even after the overthrow of the pro-Saudi monarchy of King Farouk in 1952. The new ruler of Egypt, President Gamal Abdel Nasser, was anti-Western and antimonarchy, but initially tried to maintain good relations with the Saudis.

THE DEATH OF IBN SAUD AND THE STRUGGLE FOR STABILITY

King Ibn Saud died on November 9, 1953. His final years had been unhappy, as the changes brought by oil revenues outstripped the king's ability to manage them. Still living in the same kind of mud brick palace as his ancestors, Ibn Saud's kingdom was rapidly moving beyond the informal sheikdom its founder had forged in the early twentieth century. By the late 1940s, the strong warrior, who had won his kingdom through conquest and charisma, was an old man, with arthritis in his legs and few joys left in his life. Even as his mind began a subtle decline, losing the sharpness of his early years, he still retained a tight grip on power, refusing to delegate to his brothers, sons, or advisers even the most mundane decisions. His death in 1953 came as a relief to some in the royal family, as there was hope that long-deferred important decisions might actually be made.

Although Abd al Aziz's rule had been personal and mercurial, he left behind him at least the beginnings of a government, with institutions, some technical capacity, and the beginnings of a national infrastructure. Although its infrastructure was still very basic compared to many other countries in the region, Saudi Arabia in 1953 had its first airports, roads, universities, armed forces, and a national budget, derived primarily from foreign royalties paid for Saudi petroleum. While these institutions were weak in comparison to other Arab and developing states, and far more dependent on the person of the monarch than was practical, the contrast with the loosely governed state of 1932 was phenomenal.

Abd al Aziz's death left the kingdom in the hands of his son, Saud, whose rule was ratified in late 1953 by the royal family and the ulama. However, Saud's wasteful spending, inefficient rule, and unpopularity quickly created an opposition among the Saudi princes and the population at large.

Saud and members of the royal family spent lavishly on themselves. The new king built 25 palaces for himself and maintained a court of more than 5,000 attendants, servants, slaves, and concubines. Saud tolerated corruption on a wide scale by the princes, and spent so much money on personal indulgences that Saudi Arabia, which received a dramatic increase in royalties after new arrangements with Aramco in 1950, was accumulating debt at an alarming rate. Saudi debt, which had risen to $200 million by the death of Ibn Saud in 1953, had more than doubled, to over $400 million, by 1958.

The 1950s and early 1960s witnessed a power struggle within the Saudi family over the future of the kingdom, with Saud and Faisal alternating on the throne and in key political positions. While Saud received support from traditionalists within the regime, his half-brother Faisal was an advocate for modernization and more efficiency in the use of Saudi oil revenues. Unlike Saud, who had been raised in luxurious surroundings, Faisal's younger years had been Spartan ones, given his mother's efforts to instill in the young prince the values of Abd al Wahhab, a direct ancestor of the family. Saud attempted to maintain the loyalty of tribal leaders through largesse, offering the equivalent of massive bribes—ranging from thousands to millions of dollars—in exchange for acquiescence to his rule. Tribes loyal to him also received the sinecures of state jobs and positions within the military and security services. By the late 1950s, the royal currency was rapidly losing ground against the dollar, further depleting the treasury and Saudi access to international credit.

Even as the state's finances declined, the royal family, resident Westerners, and favored tribes, who also received preferential hiring into the petroleum industry, continued to experience rising living standards and all the comforts of the modern world. At the same time, most Saudi citizens derived little or no benefits from the state, enduring the same grinding poverty and tenuous economy as their ancestors. The difference was that, for the first time, the Saudi rulers did not share the same conditions as their subjects, instead living in a world of palaces, imported luxuries, and Western travel. King Saud was indifferent to or uninterested in domestic calls for reform, instead reacting harshly against strikes, such as those that took place among Aramco workers in 1953 and 1958, and forbidding Saudi students abroad from taking classes in law, political science, or other fields that might encourage excessively critical thinking.

THE RISE OF KING FAISAL

In 1958, members of the royal family forced King Saud to cede executive power to Crown Prince Faisal, while allowing Saud to remain monarch.

Faisal's reforms, including introducing a balanced budget, ending the princes' ability to use public funds for private use, rescheduling Saudi Arabia's international debts, and otherwise introducing planning and modern accounting methods to the budget, improved the state's fiscal position within two years. Saud, however, was upset at reductions in his subsidy, and in 1961 forced Faisal to resign as prime minister. Faisal remained popular, however, and the ulama forced Saud to reinstate him as prime minister in 1962. In 1964, while the king was on a long and expensive foreign tour, the ulama and royal family reduced Saud's powers once again, leading the king to try to gather support from his traditional allies for a purge of Faisal.

After this effort failed, in late 1964, Saud abdicated and fled to exile in Europe, leaving Faisal on the throne with sole power. Although a strong believer in the traditions of the Saudi family, Faisal realized that the state had to modernize and adopt responsible fiscal measures, rather than continuing to operate on the feudal and personality-driven system of his father, Abd al Aziz, and Saud, the deposed king. For all of his reformist actions, Faisal remained a traditional monarch, meeting almost every week to consult with the ulama, holding routine audiences, open to any citizen, and arguing that the kingdom's legitimacy derived from its role as guardian of Mecca and Medina, the birthplace of the Prophet Muhammad and of the Islamic faith.

The key difference in the reign of King Faisal was in his allocation of oil revenues. While members of the royal family still had access to tremendous amounts of money, the new king made the progress of Saudi Arabia's infrastructure the highest priority. He began a series of five-year development plans, investing billions in education, transportation, industry, and other areas to improve the economy and raise living standards for Saudi families. Faisal administered these programs through a new Central Planning Organization, hiring economists, accountants, businessmen, and management professionals to oversee his ambitious plans. For example, he focused major development programs on welfare state measures, beginning a national social insurance system in 1969 and initiating in 1970 a plan to build hospitals, train physicians and other medical professionals, and improve access to basic health services throughout the nation. King Faisal also introduced free education for all Saudi male subjects, including at the university level. Approximately 10 percent of the annual budget was devoted to public education at all levels, including funds for Saudi students to study abroad, necessary to compensate for the inadequacies of domestic higher education in capacity and capability.

The biggest expenditures, however, were for the military, with spending on the Saudi armed forces typically taking the largest percentage—40 percent—of the national budget. Faisal designated one of his half-brothers, Sultan, as defense minister, charged with the responsibility to create a modern military. The new oil wealth of Saudi Arabia made possible many things, but it also made the nation's territory an attractive target for foreign powers. Given the vulnerability of Saudi oil fields to air attack, Defense Minister Sultan invested heavily in air defense systems, purchased aircraft from the United States, and began to create a Western-style army to defend the nation's borders against potential threats. Given the hostility of Saudi Arabia to Egypt, the Soviet Union, Iraq, Iran, and other states active in the region, the military was not without real or potential threats. Ongoing internal dissent, from disadvantaged tribes as well as out-of-favor royal princes, also motivated Faisal to give high priority to Sultan's efforts.

King Faisal also continued the modernization of the political system, creating a Ministry of Justice in 1970 to standardize legal codes, and to supervise the administration of justice and the courts. On the cultural front, King Faisal also permitted several measures that were controversial in deeply conservative Saudi Arabia, including the education of women and the introduction of television. Even though many Saudis opposed these changes, including those who protested against Riyadh's first television station in 1965, King Faisal's increasing control over the ulama ensured compliance.

CONFLICTS IN THE ARAB WORLD

Saudi foreign policy had been conservative from the beginning. Hesitant to be drawn into foreign wars, Ibn Saud had been a reluctant participant in World War II, and had not deployed forces into that conflict or even into the several Arab-Israeli conflicts. Although generally supportive of Arab wars against Israel, it was unwilling to risk its economic ties to the West through a broader involvement. Usually cautious in its foreign relations, the Saudis tried to support Arab gains in the international arena, without risking itself. For example, in 1956, Saudi Arabia initially supported Egypt's seizure of the Suez Canal, and even severed ties to Britain and France, but refused to send military aid when Israel, France, and the United Kingdom attacked the Egyptians. By the late 1950s, Saudi Arabia had become increasingly disturbed by the radical socialism and Arab nationalism promoted by Egypt's Nasser.

In 1957, Saudi Arabia signed defensive agreements with the conservative Hashemite monarchies of Jordan and Iraq, despite long-standing enmity over past struggles to control Arabia. Also during this period, the Saudis began to finance internal and external propaganda campaigns against communism, Arab nationalism, and socialism, viewing them as serious threats to the survival of the monarchy. Saudi Arabia also reversed its tentative distancing of itself from the United States. In February 1957, King Saud visited President Eisenhower, and agreed to extend American use of the Dhahran air base for five years, in exchange for U.S. military aid and training. This visit and these concessions were unpopular in much of the Arab world, especially so soon after the 1956 Suez crisis and war, but the Saudis viewed the U.S. alliance as vital for survival. Saudi efforts did not yield the expected increases in security, as when the alliance with Iraq collapsed after a military coup overthrew 18-year-old King Faisal II in 1958, leading to a nationalistic and pan-Arab military dictatorship under General Abd al-Karim Qasim.

Despite this opposition to Nasserite values and communism, the Saudi monarchy did not have the military resources or political will to confront Egypt or other pan-Arab states directly. Instead, Saudi intervention came only when it felt allied regimes threatened, and even then, its involvement was primarily financial and diplomatic. In 1958, Saudi Arabia financed an assassination plot against Egypt's Nasser, a botched effort that became a humiliating failure when the news became public. King Saud's popularity, already in decline because of his financial mismanagement, collapsed among the royal family and Saudi population, leading to his abdication. After the failed assassination, the first major example of broader intervention came in 1962, when the traditional imamate monarchy of Yemen fell to a Nasserite group of intellectuals and officers, who declared the Yemen Arab Republic, and became allies of Egypt. Fearing that Nasserite ideas might spread elsewhere in the peninsula, the Saudi kingdom sent money and technical aid to supporters of the traditional Yemeni imam. Even though the Yemeni imam led a sect of Shia Islam, this religious difference was less of a threat than rising pan-Arabism and socialism.

For the next eight years, the Saudis remained embroiled in the conflict, as their Yemeni royalist allies fought republicans allied to Egypt, and as many as 60,000 members of Egypt's armed forces, which employed armor, helicopters, and even chemical weapons. Although republican forces won in 1970, the long standoff had weakened Nasserism, and the Egyptian leader died the same year. Although Saudi Arabia's allies lost the war, the conflict demonstrated the growing determination of the kingdom to assert its influence in the region. The government of the Yemen Arab Republic became more conservative in the years that followed, and in 1973, Saudi Arabia and Yemen revived the Treaty of Taif, which had originally established the borders between the two states in 1934. Egypt and Saudi Arabia, despite their conflicts, also forged closer ties after the death of Nasser, as exemplified by the visit of King Faisal to Egypt in 1971.

Saudi Arabia opposed the creation of the state of Israel, but did not send more than token forces to fight in the Arab-Israeli Wars. In 1967, the Saudi state even declared neutrality in the Six-Day War, preferring not to support what it saw as Nasser's conflict against the Israelis, calculated to gain prestige for the Egyptian leader. Even though it remained militarily removed from these wars, its major contribution to these efforts was financial, in the form of organized boycotts and oil embargoes against Western nations seen as supportive of Israel. King Faisal slowly raised Saudi Arabia's stature among the other Arab states and the developing world, extending humanitarian aid and diplomatic support to Islamic causes, while trying to avoid being seen as too radical by its Western commercial partners, especially the United States.

A consistent enemy of Israel, King Faisal provided support to Palestinian refugees, collaborated with Kuwait and Libya to subsidize Jordan and Egypt after their 1967 defeat by Israel, and in 1973 recognized the Palestine Liberation Organization (PLO) of Chairman Yasser Arafat as the legitimate representative of all Palestinians, in exile or living under Israeli occupation. An umbrella organization of several distinct Palestinian factions, the PLO included representatives from the refugee and exile communities throughout the region. This was the height of the PLO's international prominence, as its use of terrorism gained it international media attention. King Faisal also promised to support the PLO financially, pledging approximately $300 million annually to the organization.

OPEC AND THE GULF STATES

By the late 1950s, many oil-producing states, including Saudi Arabia, began to question their long-standing financial arrangements with Western petroleum companies. In the Saudi case, the royal family became increasingly unhappy that Aramco was making more profit from oil exports than the government of Saudi Arabia. This discontent led Saudi Arabia to participate in the founding of the Organization of Petroleum Exporting States (OPEC) in 1960, along with Iran, Iraq, Kuwait, and Venezuela. Other states soon joined, and the organization commanded a dominating share of world oil production. Beginning in the late 1960s, OPEC nations, including Saudi Arabia, renegotiated royalty arrangements with Western oil companies. Saudi Arabia signed an agreement with Aramco that gave it an increasing stake in the company, rising to 25 percent by 1973.

Despite a common economic interest in high but stable oil prices, Saudi Arabia often clashed in the 1970s with other OPEC members, especially more radical regimes such as Libya, Iraq, and Algeria. While these governments advocated a harsher line against Western states, including continuing the 1973 oil boycott and measures to exact higher prices, Saudi oil ministers and executives argued that oil's utility as a weapon was limited. A boycott could lead to conservation and a determined search for alternatives, while low petroleum prices ensured ongoing Western dependence on Middle Eastern crude oil. The ease of extracting Saudi oil also militated in favor of larger production volumes, since the profit point was lower for Aramco than for any other national oil company or foreign concession.

CONCLUSION

Saudi Arabia by the early 1970s was almost unrecognizable as the state that had officially taken this name in 1932. The tremendous oil assets—25 percent of the known global reserves—underneath the sands of Saudi Arabia had literally fueled the leapfrogging of the country from abject poverty to fantastic wealth in one generation. Fundamentally, however, Saudi Arabia's prosperity was fragile, dependent as it was on the relative scarcity of petroleum in the world, as well as on Aramco's comparative advantage on extraction costs. Saudi oil revenues also exposed a paradox: the more money spent by the state on education, infrastructure, and other benefits for its people, the more expensive the government was, and dependent on increasing oil revenues to maintain this system of social welfare and domestic development. Absent a truly diverse economy, something that eluded the rulers of Saudi Arabia despite their efforts, Saudi Arabia remained subject to the dramatic swings of international commodity pricing.

Despite this vulnerability, Saudi Arabia, especially under Crown Prince, and later King, Faisal developed into an increasingly modern state during the 1960s and 1970s. Rich, influential, and enjoying domestic peace, at least in regional comparison, Saudi Arabia had by the end of this period established a functioning government, capable of delivering basic services to most of its citizens, and gaining in capacity with every new development plan. The late 1970s and the decades that followed, however, would present Saudi Arabia with unprecedented challenges, both from internal and international threats, and would test the monarchy as never before. At the same time extremely vulnerable and surprisingly stable, Saudi Arabia survived these events, but in many cases at seemingly unbearable financial and social cost. The persistence of the regime during the last decades of the twentieth century and into the twenty-first serves as testament to the resiliency of the monarchy established by Ibn Saud, but is no guarantee of future survival in one of the world's most volatile and dangerous regions.

8

Saudi Arabia in the Modern World (1973–2006)

In the last quarter of the twentieth century, Saudi Arabia's economy, international role, and importance to the West rose to unparalleled heights. Fueled by global demand for crude oil, and led by a succession of mostly able monarchs and crown princes, the Saudi state modernized and adapted to rapidly changing circumstances, both foreign and domestic. Despite success in raising living standards and Saudi Arabia's global profile, underlying stresses caused by domestic religious conflicts, regional wars, the inefficiencies of the economy, the relationship to the West, the status of foreign workers, and the threat of terrorism confronted the royal government and its subjects. Saudi involvement in military activities, including massive arms purchases, issuing loans to Saddam Hussein during the Iran-Iraq War, and hosting hundreds of thousands of foreigners during the Gulf War, also added to domestic questions over the role of Saudi Arabia in the world.

The presence of 25 percent of the world's known reserves of crude oil underneath the soil of Saudi Arabia meant that internal developments had immediate international significance. The connection between oil and politics was never as essential in the rise of a nation as it was during the 1970s, when Saudi Arabia transformed. At the beginning of this period, Saudi Arabia was a state taken for granted as a supplier of an essential global commodity, along with its role as the birthplace of Islam and site of the religion's two holiest cities. By the middle of the decade, and into the years that followed, it had become a nation whose counsel, financial resources, and political agenda had to be taken seriously as a leader by the Arab world, the United States, Western nations, and rest of the globe.

OIL POLITICS IN THE 1970s

OPEC, which had been founded in 1960, was by the early 1970s a powerful intergovernmental organization, with a controlling interest in global oil production. Member states committed to production quotas, ensuring that global oil prices would not fall too low. Especially after the Arab defeat in 1967's Six-Day War, and the Israeli occupation of the West Bank, Gaza Strip, Golan Heights, and Jerusalem, many Arab states began to consider the use of one of their only remaining assets—oil—as a weapon against the United States, Israel's most important ally. Arab states in OPEC had attempted to impose an embargo in 1967, but a global oil glut had caused this effort to fail. By the early 1970s, the United States was also much more dependent on foreign oil, and global demand had grown.

On October 6, Egypt and Syria launched a surprise attack on Israel. The United States asked King Faisal to encourage the Arab states to end the war, but the Saudi ruler refused, hoping the conflict would end in an Israeli withdrawal from occupied Arab territory. After President Nixon granted over $2 billion in aid to Israel, despite American promises of neutrality in the conflict, Faisal resolved to take action and declared a unilateral embargo on oil shipments to the United States and the Netherlands, which had also supported the Israelis.

On October 19, 1973, the Arab states within OPEC voted to support Saudi Arabia and impose an oil embargo on the United States and other Western nations that had supported Israel in the 1973 Arab-Israeli war. This action came as a shock in the West, which had relied on a steady supply of cheap oil from the Middle East since World War II. Saudi Arabia, although not an active participant in the 1973 war, supported this action. Gas prices doubled, then tripled, as OPEC nations limited, and then cut off, sales to the United States, which was already in the midst of an economic downturn. By January 1974, the price of crude oil in international commodity markets had more than tripled, from $3 to $11 per barrel.

Believing that the embargo was not achieving its goal of ending U.S. support to Israel, and hoping that the United States might encourage the Israelis to withdraw from its occupied territories, OPEC ended the embargo in March 1974. King Faisal had supported the embargo, having lost patience with the U.S.-Israeli alliance. Several months before the 1973 war, the king had stated that he did not believe a strong relationship with the United States could persist alongside American support to Israel. An outspoken enemy of Zionism, which he linked to communism in public speeches and private meetings, he only reluctantly allowed American Jews, including U.S. Secretary of State Henry Kissinger, to visit the kingdom. Faisal aggravated foreign visitors and even some of his aides with his belief in promoting "The Protocols of the Elders of Zion," a tsarist forgery from the early twentieth century that purported to detail a global Jewish conspiracy to control the world.

SAUDI ARABIA AND THE ARAB WORLD

Saudi Arabia's leadership of the embargo transformed its position among the Arab states. Not only did Riyadh gain increased legitimacy in the Middle East for its resistance to the United States in the 1973 war, the embargo dramatically increased Saudi oil revenues, as prices never returned to prewar levels. Pre-1973 budgets under King Faisal had been austere, but throughout the rest of the 1970s and early 1980s, Saudi revenues increased from $10 billion to nearly $200 billion. While inflation had some impact on these funds, the Saudi kingdom nonetheless had tens of billions to spend on internal development, military spending, international aid, and other national priorities.

Despite the tensions involved in the Arab oil boycott, by spring 1974 the United States and Saudi Arabia had begun to repair relations. Kissinger's role in mediating a ceasefire between Israel and the Arabs, as well as the Saudi kings' concerns about radicalism in the Arab world, encouraged this rapprochement. King Faisal threatened to leave OPEC if the other states did not end the embargo, and in June 1974, President Nixon became the first U.S. president to visit Saudi Arabia. The United States and Saudi Arabia negotiated a 60 percent share for the Saudi government in Aramco, accelerating already rapidly rising Saudi oil revenues. Faisal's image rose throughout the world, and at the end of 1974 *Time* magazine declared him their "Man of the Year." In 10 years, he had transformed Saudi Arabia from the feudal state of Abd al Aziz and Saud into a modernizing state, rich, influential, and developing rapidly. Unlike his predecessors, Faisal's was not a personal state, dependent for all decisions on the king. Instead, he had appointed the most competent princes and other Saudi citizens, many of them Western-educated, to key ministries and positions throughout the kingdom.

REIGN OF KING FAHD

On March 25, 1975, a nephew at the monarch's weekly public audience assassinated King Faisal. Crown Prince Khalid became king, and appointed Prince Fahd as his successor. Khalid was not an active king, however, preferring to leave the daily operations of government in the hands of Fahd. The late 1970s were a time of unprecedented wealth in Saudi Arabia, and characterized by massive public investments in infrastructure, education, health, and agriculture. A pious and private man, Khalid was generally popular, and benefited from the unparalleled prosperity of his kingdom. The death of King Khalid in 1982, after a series of heart problems, allowed Crown Prince Fahd to take the throne and rule in his own name, as he had been doing on behalf of Khalid since 1975.

Unprecedented wealth enabled the monarchy to expand the state apparatus dramatically. Between 1972 and 1977, annual oil revenues to the government increased from just under $2 billion to over $40 billion. While there was some downward fluctuation in the mid-1980s, as oil prices fell during the Iran-Iraq War, Saudi Arabia continued to have billions of petrodollars available to meet its financial priorities: infrastructure, the armed forces, health, education, foreign aid, and spending by the thousands of members of the extended royal family and its affiliated tribes. Especially in the 1970s, the government earned so much from Aramco and other oil companies that it was unable to spend all of its revenues domestically, instead investing billions of dollars in the United States and other overseas markets. These surpluses allowed the government of Saudi Arabia, as well as its wealthiest citizens, to spend lavishly on luxury homes, yachts, and other forms of conspicuous consumption both at home and overseas, especially in Europe and the United States.

One side effect of the wealth of the Saudi state, developing against the backdrop of a relatively undereducated and low-skilled population, was that there were not enough workers in the domestic labor force to provide for the needs of a modern economy. While foreign workers, especially other Arabs, had long played a minor role in the Saudi economy as professionals, or as visitors on pilgrimage who had remained permanently in the Hijaz, oil wealth and the boom in national expenditures dramatically increased this expatriate presence. Additionally, many Saudi citizens gravitated to positions within the government, especially in the state bureaucracy or security forces, leaving both menial and technical positions unfilled. Low levels of education, especially at the postsecondary level, meant that there were not enough native doctors, engineers, scientists, and other professionals to fill needed positions in the oil and affiliated industries. The majority of teachers, especially at the secondary and postsecondary level, were also foreigners, especially other Arabs.

At the other end of the vocational scale, traditional Saudi culture discouraged men from taking jobs as manual laborers, and there was also strong pressure against women working, and in many cases bans on them serving in entire professions. Women could only work in professions where they would not interact with men who were not related by blood or marriage, and so were limited to occupations such as teaching and working in family businesses. Prohibitions against women driving also severely limited their options, as did the requirement that they receive explicit permission from their father or husband to continue in employment outside the home or family enterprise. Unwilling to tap its female population for workers, and thereby sidelining half of the Saudi population from the job market, the Saudi government had little choice but to import foreign male workers for its industries, as well as an army of female domestic servants to work for Saudi women in the home.

By the early 1970s, foreigners accounted for over 50 percent of the work force in Saudi Arabia. While foreign workers had to receive government permits to receive official status, many remained in the country illegally. By the mid-1970s, there were over two million foreigners in Saudi Arabia, although less than half of these had applied for legal residency. Although the guest workers came from dozens of countries, and the government did not maintain reliable statistics, there were three main groups: Americans and Europeans worked primarily as engineers and managers for Aramco, thousands of Arabs, especially Egyptians, Palestinians, and Jordanians, worked as professionals, while Yemenis and South Asians worked as menial labor in industry, agriculture, and domestic service. The highest concentrations of foreigners were in the Hijaz, the traditional commercial and pilgrimage zone in the West, and in the oil-rich Eastern Province along the Persian Gulf.

Underneath the wealth and construction, there were danger signs that all was not well in the peninsula. Traditionalists, religious students, members of tribes that had been excluded from government largesse, affiliates of the fundamentalist Muslim Brotherhood, and some members of the military, especially those descended from the purged Ikhwan military order, believed the monarchy had become too decadent and pro-Western. One faction, the Movement of Muslim Revolutionaries of the Arabian Peninsula (MMRAP), took action in November 1979. Two MMRAP groups attempted to seize control of Medina and Mecca. While government and police crushed the attack on Medina, a force of up to 1,000 rebels took control of Mecca's Grand Mosque on November 20. Crown Prince Fahd, supported by a fatwa from Saudi religious scholars that declared the rebels' action unjustified, ordered an assault on the mosque. After two weeks of fighting, government forces killed or captured the last MMRAP insurgents, at a cost of almost 500 dead in both cities, as well as damage to the Grand Mosque and other sites. Even though the monarchy was able to reassert control, the incident was a tremendous embarrassment to King Khalid, who derived his much of his legitimacy from his role of protector of Mecca and Medina, and the requirement that he keep these cities open for pilgrimage by Muslims.

Just as the Saudi government was completing its defeat of the MMRAP, unrest spread to the Shia minority in the Eastern Province. Long persecuted by the Saudi state and prohibited from practicing their faith openly, in late 1979 and early 1980, Saudi Shia began to protest, demanding religious freedom to honor their saints. Emboldened by the 1979 Iranian Revolution, which had overthrown the Shah and brought the Ayatollah Khomeini into power at the head of a Shia religious state, the Saudi Shia began demonstrations. Although Iran did not play a direct role in the uprising, its state radio encouraged the movement, increasing fears in Saudi Arabia that the Ayatollah's movement could spread. As with the assault on the Grand Mosque, Prince Fahd used police and army units to crush the Shia movement, which in any case never rose to the level of violence in Mecca.

Ever conscious of his role as protector of Islam's two holiest sites, in 1986 King Fahd took the formal title Custodian of the Two Holy Mosques, and in the late 1980s embarked on a multibillion program to modernize the infra-structure of the two cities. His intent was to demonstrate that the Saudi mon-archy remained committed to the annual hajj pilgrimage, and was worthy of continuing as guarantors of Islam's birthplace, after the MMRAP uprising of 1979, an Iranian riot in 1987 that resulted in over 400 deaths, and other inci-dents. At Fahd's direction, the two cities built roads and pedestrian walkways, improved security, expanded worship areas, improved air conditioning, and completed drainage and other utility work to accommodate tens of thousands more pilgrims at one time.

Fears of Iran and anger at the Soviet Union's 1979 invasion of Afghanistan accelerated Saudi ties with the United States. Although the United States had sold Saudi Arabia over $30 billion in armaments during the 1970s, including a controversial sale of F-15s under the presidency of Jimmy Carter, these pur-chases increased dramatically after 1980. In that year, Iraq invaded Iran, thus beginning a major war in the Persian Gulf area. Iraq's Arab leader, Saddam Hussein, hoped to take advantage of the tumult caused by the Iranian revo-lution to seize territory from the Iranians, as well as to raise his standing in the Islamic world. Proposed Saudi purchases of advanced weaponry initially concerned supporters of Israel within the United States, but indirect Saudi diplomacy assured Israel that these weapons would be primarily defensive in nature. While Saudi Arabia and Israel remained officially at war, the fighter jets, airborne AWACs radar systems, and air defense systems purchased with Saudi oil revenues were clearly focused against the Soviet Union and Iran, both outspoken enemies of the Jewish state, which were also seen as signifi-cant threats to Saudi oil fields during the decade.

The Iran-Iraq War increased Saudi concerns about their security. Although relations between secular Iraq and Saudi Arabia had never been warm, the monarchy recognized that revolutionary Iran was a far greater threat to its survival and the stability of the region, and immediately lent its support, and significant financial resources, to the Iraqi campaign. The Saudi government loaned or guaranteed over $25 billion to Saddam's regime, and encouraged other Gulf States, including Kuwait, Bahrain, and the United Arab Emirates, to do the same. The war, expected to result in a quick Iraqi victory, rapidly bogged down in the marshy terrain of the Shatt-al-Arab, where the Tigris and Euphrates converge near the Persian Gulf. Saudi Arabia dramatically raised its oil production to cover the costs of the war, as well as to weaken Iran's ability to fund its campaigns. While this measure did have the desired impact on Iran, it also cost the Saudi government billions in revenue, as oil prices plunged from over $30 a barrel to less than $15 by the mid-1980s. The United Nations-brokered truce that ended the war in late 1988 left massive destruction in the region, and left Iraq chafing at demands by the Gulf States that it begin repaying the estimated $40 billion it had borrowed during the conflict, principally from Saudi Arabia and Kuwait.

Saudi Arabia was also the chief financial backer of the mujahideen, Afghan rebels who rose up to fight against the Soviet occupation in the 1980s. In cooperation with Pakistan, and with covert assistance from the United States, the Saudis spent billions on weapons and training for the mujahideen. The kingdom also provided humanitarian aid for the estimated five million Afghan refugees in Pakistan. One unanticipated result of this funding was the creation of a regional network of fanatical fighters in the 1980s, including the wealthy Saudi construction heir, Osama bin Laden. While the initial fervor of these jihadist fighters was directed at the Soviet Union in the 1980s, the withdrawal of Soviet forces in 1988–1989 left behind a new organization, Al Qaeda (The Base), dedicated to the continuation of jihad against other enemies, including Saudi Arabia and the West.

GULF WAR

On August 2, 1990, Iraq invaded neighboring Kuwait, hoping to annex the emirate as its 19th province, seize its oil fields, and use its $100 billion in financial reserves to pay down its debt and rebuild from the Iran-Iraq War. Terrified of the more than 100,000 Iraqi soldiers massed in Kuwait, on August 6, King Fahd invited the United States to deploy military forces in defense of Saudi Arabia. By the end of 1990, over 500,000 American and other coalition forces, including Egyptians and Syrians, were in Saudi Arabia preparing to expel the Iraqis from Kuwait if negotiations failed. Operation Desert Shield, as the defensive effort was called by the United States, was very unpopular in Saudi Arabia. Saudi subjects began to question the billions that had been spent on defense in previous years. If the Saudi armed forces could not defend the nation against external threats, then why spend so much on armaments, foreign advisers, and the salaries of hundreds of thousands of military personnel?

Other Saudis were angry about the arrival of hundreds of thousands of foreigners on their territory, believing they would corrupt Islamic values and defile the land that was the birthplace of the Prophet Muhammad. Many fundamentalist Saudis were upset about the presence of Christian and Jewish U.S. military chaplains, American females in uniform, and other un-Islamic practices. While U.S. commander General Norman Schwarzkopf tried to appease Saudi public opinion through issuing orders forbidding alcohol, prohibiting pornography among the soldiers, and limiting entertainment, including USO shows, to events that would not offend, there were inevitable inadvertent cultural clashes. Even a fatwa by Saudi religious leaders, authorizing the temporary stationing of foreign forces in Saudi Arabia to defend Islam against a potential threat from Iraq, did little to calm domestic concerns.

Saudi Arabia portrayed its military forces as playing a primary role in the defense of its territory, with plans for the liberation of Kuwait. The United States agreed that a prominent Arab role was necessary for the legitimacy of the coalition, and supported the appointment of Major General Khaled bin Sultan, son of the Saudi Minister of Defense, as commander of the Arab forces: principally Saudis, Syrians, and Egyptians, but also affiliated units from the Gulf Cooperation Council and even some Kuwaitis who had escaped the Iraqi invasion. The Saudi-led force received the honor of officially liberating Kuwait, although the bulk of offensive operations were conducted by other coalition forces.

CRISIS OF THE 1990s

The rapid coalition victory over Saddam Hussein in early 1991 did little to minimize Saudi anger at the monarch. Saudi expenditures on behalf of the coalition forces, including paying for all fuel, bottled water, and other supplies, cost over $50 billion, and created a budget deficit for the first time in many years. Domestic anger at foreign bases did not end with the expulsion of Iraq from Kuwait, particularly as the United States maintained a permanent presence in Saudi Arabia after the end of the Gulf War, with more than 5,000 U.S. Air Force and Army personnel stationed in the kingdom, mostly in the Eastern Province near the Persian Gulf. From these Saudi bases, U.S. forces policed the "no-fly zones" over Iraq, monitored Iranian activity, and maintained a strong presence in the region. The ongoing basing of "infidels" in the home of Mecca and Medina became a point of resentment, and a recruiting tool, for anti-Western movements in the Middle East, including Al Qaeda, which remained based in Afghanistan, Sudan, and Pakistan in the 1990s.

Contributing to the crisis in Saudi Arabia was the ongoing global oil glut, which caused prices to remain below $20 a barrel throughout most of the

1990s. With the conventional threats posed by Iraq and Iran diminished, and OPEC states violating their own quota system in pursuit of quick profits, worldwide oil production increased even as Western nations and Japan experienced recessions or slow economic growth. Faced with this reduced demand and greatly increased supply, the Saudi budget operated with perpetual annual deficits of $20 billion, and per capita income fell by more than 50 percent, to just over $7,000 by the mid-1990s. A country that had been unable to spend its surpluses in the 1970s and early 1980s had become one characterized by austerity, recession, and declining living standards, a series of events blamed by fundamentalists on the Saudi monarchy's close collaboration with the United States and other Western nations.

King Fahd attempted to manage the multiple crises of the 1990s with modest reforms, crackdowns on dissent, and international engagement to rehabilitate Saudi Arabia's image. The most important reforms, announced in 1992, were the creation of the Basic Law, the Consultative Council, and the Law of the Provinces. The Basic Law established the rules for succession, reasserted Saudi Arabia as a dynastic and Islamic kingdom under the sons and grandsons of Abd Al Aziz Al Saud, and formalized the Consultative Council. This appointive body of Saudi men, initially 60 in number, had no formal power, but was an advisory body of prestigious men who could provide recommendations and serve as a sounding board for the king and his cabinet. The Law of the Provinces confirmed and standardized the regions, strengthening the office of governor, and further subdividing the provinces into more manageable districts and precincts.

The 1990s also saw serious efforts to limit dissent within Saudi Arabia. While in previous decades, it had been liberal and reformist opposition that most concerned the government, after 1990 it was militant fundamentalism. Muslims who believed that the Saudi royal family was hopelessly corrupt, and had betrayed its obligation to protect pure Islam, began to form small groups to protest and, in some cases, take up arms against the monarchy and its Western supporters. Chief among these was Osama bin Laden, who in 1994 was stripped of his Saudi citizenship for his financing of terrorism. From his sanctuaries in Sudan and Afghanistan, he demanded the overthrow of the Saudi kingdom and its replacement with an ultraconservative revived Islamic caliphate, which would include the entire Islamic world. Domestically, the Saudi state maintained vigilance against radical clerics, establishing central authorities to supervise mosques and religious schools.

Internationally, Saudi Arabia spent generously on Islamic causes in the 1990s, hoping to restore the positive image it had in the 1970s and early 1980s. From funding madrassas (religious schools) in Pakistan, to building mosques in Western nations, to sending humanitarian aid to Northern Africa, to providing arms for the beleaguered Bosnian Muslims, Saudi aid was everywhere in the Islamic world. Western criticism accompanied much of this assistance, as the Saudi government, private citizens, and foundations heavily favored the most fundamentalist, pro-Wahhabi institutions, even forcing local Muslims to change their curriculums, methods, and other activities to reflect a more conservative interpretation of Islam. As with Saudi support for the mujahideen in the 1980s, its foreign aid efforts in the 1990s assisted in creating a more fertile ground for the spread of jihadist ideas, at odds with the official goals of the Saudi kingdom. While some members of the royal family have been more supportive of extreme versions of already fundamentalist Wahhabism, they are a minority within a basically conservative and status quo oriented hierarchy.

THE PALESTINIAN ISSUE

Saudi Arabia had long been one of the primary financial backers of the Palestinians and their primary organization, the Palestinian Liberation Organization, providing it with hundreds of millions in the 1970s, and an estimated $1 billion in the 1980s. The kingdom had also maintained its hostility to Israel, and support for the Palestinian cause, in international organizations such as the United Nations and the Arab League, and had been one of the most effective supporters of the Arab embargo against the Jewish state. In the 1960s and 1970s, tens of thousands of Palestinians had received refugee status in Saudi Arabia, especially those with technical and professional skills needed by the Saudi economy. Palestinian support for Iraq during its invasion of Kuwait, including collaborating with Iraqi security forces during the occupation of the emirate, however, had infuriated King Fahd, who cut off almost all direct financial aid to the PLO in 1991. The site of Palestinians in the West Bank, Gaza, and in refugee camps cheering for Saddam Hussein, cheering Iraqi missile launches against Saudi Arabia, and holding demonstrations against U.S.-led efforts to liberate Kuwait, were too much for the Saudi monarchy to ignore, despite the kingdom's long-standing political and financial support for the Palestinians and the PLO.

By the mid-1990s, Saudi Arabia and other members of the Gulf Cooperation Council ended their strict enforcement of the Arab anti-Israeli boycott, although they retained a ban on direct trade with Israel. In August 1993, Israel and the Palestinians signed the Oslo Accords, beginning mutual recognition, committing to an end to violence, and pledging negotiations for a final settlement. Saudi Arabia strongly supported these discussions, and pledged $100 million annually for the newly established Palestinian Authority. At the same time, still cool to the PLO, Saudi Arabia began to provide indirect aid to the radical movement Hamas, which favored an Islamist state in Palestine, and remained committed to a violent struggle against Israel. Seeing Hamas as a counterweight to the PLO, the Saudis were also encouraged by the greater piety, dedication to social justice, and lack of outward corruption and among Hamas leaders. Reflecting the Islamic foundations of the movement, Hamas leaders also displayed fewer of the vices common in the Palestinian Authority, such as nepotism and contributing to the cult of personality around Arafat. Although King Abdullah and other Saudi leaders remained troubled by the suicide bombings and other attacks employed by the movement against Israel and, increasingly, the Fatah movement of Yasser Arafat within the Palestine Liberation Organization, the Saudis hoped that the responsibility of governance might lead Hamas to become more responsible in its actions. The Saudis also expected that their financial support might wean Hamas away from its more radical sponsors, Syria and Iran, to a more moderate approach.

THE LONG DECLINE OF KING FAHD

In 1995, King Fahd suffered a stroke, and the daily operation of the government passed to Crown Prince Abdullah, the monarch's half-brother, who held the position of deputy prime minister. Although Fahd continued to reign until his death in 2005, by most accounts he did not rule, only occasionally intervening in government affairs or meeting with Saudi or foreign dignitaries. This uncertainty made major decisions difficult, as Prince Abdullah often clashed with other members of the royal family who preferred Fahd. With oil prices stagnant, the Saudi government attempted to expand into other commercial areas, including natural gas and agriculture. Also during this period, and despite initial expectations, U.S.-Saudi relations improved dramatically. The two nations collaborated in their support for ending the wars in Bosnia and Kosovo, where Muslims were under attack, and also promoted a permanent Palestinian-Israeli settlement. The failure of President Bill Clinton's effort in 2000 to broker an agreement between Arafat and Israeli Prime Minister Ehud Barak was a disappointment to both nations, especially in light of the revived Palestinian intifada, or uprising, that followed the collapse of negotiations.

The coming to office of President George W. Bush in 2001 was welcomed by Saudi Arabia. As the son of the revered George H. W. Bush, and a Texas oil man, there were great expectations for a strong relationship. By mid-2001, however, Prince Abdullah was disappointed in the new president. Bush's unwavering support for Israel, and for lack of engagement in the Middle East, caused the Saudi king to question the U.S. president's commitment and judgment. By late August, Crown Prince Abdullah was sending signals that the kingdom might have to reduce its military ties and political collaboration with the United States, if it did not take a more active and even-handed role in promoting Middle East peace. On August 29, President Bush wrote a personal letter to Abdullah, pledging support for a Palestinian state, the first time the

United States had made this position official. Encouraged, Crown Prince Abdullah shared the letter with other Arab leaders, and hope briefly revived in the region that the United States would be engaging in active diplomacy to seek a broad political settlement of the long-standing conflict between Israel and its neighbors.

9/11

On September 11, nineteen terrorists hijacked four commercial airliners, deliberately flying three of them into the World Trade Center in New York City and the Pentagon in Washington, D.C. The hijackers crashed the fourth aircraft into a field in Pennsylvania when the crew and passengers of the fourth airliner attempted to retake the plane. Almost 3,000 people died in the attacks, including all the terrorists. A wave of sympathy for the United States emerged throughout the world, but in Saudi Arabia these feelings were mixed with a sense of shock, after it was learned that 15 of the 19 hijackers were Saudi citizens, and that Al Qaeda and its leader, Osama bin Laden, had masterminded the attack. Saudi Arabia initially attempted to downplay this information, attempting to keep local media from broadcasting Saudi involvement. With the availability of satellite news in most Saudi homes, especially through the popular Qatar-based *Al Jazeera*, however, this proved impossible.

King Fahd sent a personal note to President Bush, expressing his grief and condolences, but otherwise Saudi Arabia did not take any responsibility for the acts committed by its nationals. The U.S. invasion of Afghanistan in October 2001 was deeply unpopular in Saudi Arabia, where polls showed a majority of educated Saudis were sympathetic to Al Qaeda and the Taliban, while disbelieving claims that either was responsible for 9/11. U.S.-Saudi relations continued to decline during this period, with accusations in the United States that Osama bin Laden and his Afghan allies received ongoing support from influential foundations and members of the Saudi family, if not the government itself.

Behind the scenes, Saudi Arabia collaborated in what became known in the United States as the Global War on Terrorism. Saudi officials shared intelligence with U.S. agencies, provided some assistance in shutting down Islamic charities known to be conduits for terrorist funding, froze suspect bank accounts and assets, arrested hundreds of militants, and increased surveillance of former mujahideen. Given Arab and Saudi national opinion of the United States, however, as well as the ongoing intractable Palestinian issue, there were clear limits on how far Prince Abdullah was willing go along with President Bush and his new campaign against Islamic terrorists. Saudi leaders bristled at the initial description of the American response to 9/11 as a "crusade" against terrorism, loaded as the term was with images of Western Christian knights pillaging the Middle East in the eleventh century. Fortunately for U.S.-Arab relations, by late 2001, President Bush and the rest of the U.S. government had abandoned the term "crusade" in favor of "the Global War on Terrorism."

At the annual Arab League summit, held in Beirut in March 2002, Abdullah proposed a dramatic peace initiative: the Arab states would offer normalized diplomatic relations with Israel, in exchange for a return to the 1967 borders. While there remained dramatic hurdles impending such a prospective agreement, the Saudi proposal for the first time offered Israel a chance to gain recognition by the Arab states. In April 2002, Abdullah met with Bush at the president's ranch in Texas to discuss the peace plan. After some initial enthusiasm, all sides began to back away from the plan, as the ongoing intifada, Arab insistence that all Palestinian refugees be allowed to return, and a lack of agreement over what "normalized" relations with Israel might mean, got in the way of new discussions. Despite the initial failure of the proposal, it remained the baseline for potential broader Arab-Israeli discussions, replacing previous declarations by the Arab League that there should only be one state, an Arab and Islamic one, in all of Palestine, including the territory of Israel itself.

INVASION OF IRAQ

In March 2003, the United States and its allies invaded Iraq, determined to eliminate the threat of weapons of mass destruction from the regime of Saddam Hussein, and frustrated by the Iraqi's defiance of UN arms inspections, the terms of the 1991 truce, and economic sanctions. Opinion in Saudi Arabia was almost universally against the invasion, seen as an unnecessary attack on an Arab nation. Arab satellite television focused on civilian casualties, and increased anger about the war. Despite Saudi opinion, U.S. Central Command used bases in Saudi Arabia for planning and operations in the conflict. After the defeat of the Iraqi regime in late April, the United States announced that it would withdraw virtually all of its military personnel from the kingdom, a process completed by fall 2003. Although small numbers remained in Saudi Arabia, these were almost all assigned as trainers to the Saudi military, embassy staff, and representatives working with U.S. defense contractors.

Throughout the U.S. occupation of Iraq, and even after the restoration of Iraqi sovereignty in June 2004, Saudi Arabia remained concerned about the ongoing presence of over 100,000 U.S. military personnel in Iraq, as well as the tens of thousands of additional forces in Kuwait, Bahrain, and Qatar. With the rising insurgency after 2004, however, the Saudi state no longer demanded a rapid withdrawal, fearing this would cause even greater instability and violence against the Sunni minority in Iraq. Saudi Arabia was also concerned about potential damage to its image in the West, given the large numbers of foreign fighters in Iraq who were its nationals. According to press reports, as many as 55 percent of foreign insurgents in Iraq were from Saudi Arabia, allied either with Al Qaeda or with other terrorist groups. Even higher percentages made up the suicide bombers who struck civilian and military targets with car bombs, explosive vests, and other tactics. The Iraq War forced Saudi Arabia to keep its focus on its northern border, where it stationed almost 50,000 military and security personnel, and spent over $1 billion on physical and electronic barriers to stop the flow of jihadist volunteers going in both directions.

KING ABDULLAH

In late May 2005, King Fahd's health deteriorated rapidly, and he died on August 1. Crown Prince Abdullah, who had essentially governed the state since Fahd's 1995 stroke, immediately took the throne as king and prime minister on August 1 at the age of 81. In keeping with the Basic Law and Saudi tradition, he named another half brother, Prince Sultan, as his deputy prime minister, and designated successor. As the sixth Saudi monarch, King Abdullah inherited a host of challenges, including managing volatile oil revenues, the relationship with the United States, the complexities of royal politics, and the ongoing threat of terrorism, as well as surviving in one of the most dangerous and violent regions in the world. His years as acting prime minister and crown prince had prepared him for the position, however, and many Saudis compared him to King Faisal in terms of his talents, desire for modest reforms, and image as the real power behind the throne. King Fahd, however, had been a far more effective ruler than Saud, at least before his stroke sidelined him in 1995.

As crown prince, he had gained a reputation as a modest reformer, having allowed limited municipal elections in early 2005, reorganizing the legal system, and joining the World Trade Organization in December 2005. King Abdullah also expanded the Consultative Council to 150 members and increased its role in the development of government policy, although even after these changes it remained purely advisory. Up to one-third of council seats would also eventually be chosen by election, but that reform was not immediately implemented. In 2006, Abdullah created an Allegiance Council, whose sole task was to designate the next crown prince, although Prince Sultan remained designated as Abdullah's successor. In the future, the Allegiance Council was supposed to nominate the most worthy heir to the throne, from among the direct descendants of Ibn Saud, the former king's sons and grandsons.

This reform was modest, but for the first time the succession decision was not an arbitrary one by the monarch, instead involving the chief representatives of the most important branches of Abd al Aziz's lineage. Under this new law, each king would forward the names of three nominees to the council, which would be chaired by the oldest able descendant of Abd al Aziz. The council could then vote in secret ballot, and by a two-thirds majority could approve one of the names or nominate an alternative. In the event of an impasse between the king and the Allegiance Council, after one month the council's choice would prevail. King Abdullah's hope was that this system, which also include a mechanism for declaring a king medically unfit to continue in position, would create clear guidelines for succession, rather than leaving that task to the incumbent king and his own deliberations, with the potential for open conflict within the extended royal family and its thousands of princes and competing tribal, ideological, and regional loyalties. This move was also a small step toward succession through a formal, merit-based system, rather than on informal consensus among the direct descendants of Ibn Saud. Seniority had been the primary factor in these choices, leading to increasingly old monarchs, as had been the case up to and including Crown Prince Abdullah's nomination by King Fahd.

Internationally, King Abdullah has raised Saudi Arabia's profile, attempting to forge a common Arab position on issues as diverse as Darfur, the Israeli attack on Lebanon's Hezbollah in 2006, the Palestinian conflict, human rights issues in the United Nations, and relations with Iran. With the return to higher oil prices after 9/11, and most dramatically after the U.S. invasion of Iraq, Saudi Arabia once again had the financial wherewithal to increase its foreign aid budget, pledging hundreds of millions in humanitarian and financial aid for Arab and Islamic states, as well as some non-Islamic developing nations. Among the chief recent major beneficiaries of Saudi loans and grants in the early twenty-first century have been Sunni Muslim communities in Lebanon, Afghanistan, Pakistan, and Iraq, as well as Palestinians in the Gaza Strip and the West Bank, and those living in refugee camps throughout the Middle East.

Increased oil prices restored Saudi living standards. By 2006, per capita income was once again near $14,000, yearly economic growth was 3–5 percent, the annual trade surplus stood consistently over $125 billion, and the budget surplus was $40–$50 billion. The Saudi economy began to allow more foreign investment outside the energy sector, as required after its accession to the World Trade Organization, and began to plan major privatizations as part of its economic development agenda. Although its economy continued to rely on petroleum, King Abdullah followed his predecessors' attempts to encourage diversification into agriculture, trade, construction, and even the beginnings of a tourism industry.

Despite the overall economic prosperity, Saudi Arabia under Abdullah faced significant challenges after 2006: high youth unemployment, tensions between Saudis and foreign workers, and the difficulties of continuing with a reform agenda without going too fast, thereby causing resentment among conservative Muslims, or too slow, risking alienation of reformers and the West. The reality of King Abdullah's advanced age confronted the kingdom also, as the question of succession, of critical importance in the absolute monarchy, loomed increasingly large in the minds of the Saudi royal family and those subject to its rule.

Notable People in the History of Saudi Arabia

Ishmael. Biblical son of Abraham by his handmaiden Hagar. According to Hebrew and Islamic traditions, he was the father of the Arab people. Muslims also consider him the legendary founder of Mecca and an ancestor of Muhammad.

Antigonus I. He was a Hellenistic king who attacked the Nabataean Arabs in 312 B.C., initially conquering Petra. His initial victories led to defeat, however, as his withdrawal was slowed by plunder. After these battles, Greeks and Arabs established an informal truce, lasting for over 150 years.

Aretas IV, king of the Nabataeans from 9 B.C. to 40 A.D. As a Roman client, he improved diplomatic relations with the surrounding states, expanded into the Arabian Peninsula, increased trade with the Romans, improved irrigation, and built major monuments in the capital of Petra.

Philip—Roman Emperor (r. 244–249 A.D.). As the only Arab emperor, Philip continued the era of Arab ascendancy within the empire, a brief period that began with the reign of Septimus Severus (r. 193–211). Philip, from the northern city of Shahba near Damascus, negotiated peace with the Persians and presided over the commemoration of Rome's thousandth anniversary. Philip's murder in 249 ended Arab preeminence in Rome.

Sheikh Qusay (r. 460–480 A.D.). He was a tribal leader, the original organizer of the Quraysh tribe, founder of the town of Mecca, and advocate of the Ka'bah as a site for pilgrimage. Qusay also organized a consultative council of elders, established a tradition of service for pilgrims, and was an ancestor of the Prophet Muhammad.

Khadijah bint Khawaylid (565–623 A.D.). First wife of the Prophet Muhammad. A wealthy widow of a Meccan merchant, she controlled a significant part of the caravan trade between Syria, the Hijaz, and Yemen. In 595, she hired Muhammad to manage her caravans, and shortly thereafter the two married. She was also the first woman to convert to Islam, following the example of her husband. Until her death, she was Muhammad's only wife.

Muhammad. Prophet of Islam. Muhammad was born in 570 A.D., in the caravan and pilgrimage center of Mecca. Orphaned at a young age, he was of modest means until age 25, when he married the wealthy widow Khadijah, who was 15 years his senior. At the age of 40 (610 A.D.), Muhammad had a vision in the desert, and began to receive the words of the Quran from the Angel Gabriel. With this divine inspiration, he began preaching strict monotheism in Mecca, a message that enraged the merchant class then dominant in the city, which depended on religious pilgrims to the city. Fleeing persecution, Muhammad took refuge in the city of Medina. After several years of intermittent warfare, Muhammad and his new faith, Islam, returned peacefully to take possession of Mecca in 630. He died in June 632, but not before consolidating control over much of western Arabia.

Abu Bakr al-Siddiq (573–634 A.D.). He was Muhammad's father-in-law, and after the death of the Prophet in 632, was named caliph (successor) by a council of prominent Muslims in Mecca. He had been a close companion of Muhammad's, and the fourth convert to Islam. After becoming caliph, he fought many battles within Arabia against tribes that attempted to leave the Islamic community after the death of Muhammad, and also launched expeditions against the Byzantines and Sassanian Persians.

Uthman ibn Affan (580–656 A.D.). He became the third caliph in 644 A.D. His reign saw the final written compilation of the Quran, the capture of the last Persian emperor in 651, but the end of exclusive Arab expansion and control over Islam. Accused of tolerating corruption and nepotism, Uthman was murdered by a mob in Medina in 656.

Ali ibn Abu Talib (599–661 A.D.). Muhammad's cousin and son-in-law. He became the fourth caliph, and the first imam and founder of Shia Islam, or shia t' Ali (party of Ali, or Shia), the second largest denomination within Islam. He was born in Mecca, and was close to Muhammad, converting at the age of 10.

One of the Prophet's companions, he remained loyal to him through the early years of struggle. Many of Muhammad's relatives believed that he should have been accepted as the leader of the Islamic community at the death of the Prophet. He did become caliph in 656, but was murdered in 661. He is revered by all Shia Muslims.

Mu'awiyah ibn-abi-Sufyan (602–680 A.D.). Founder of the Umayyad Dynasty. Born in Mecca around 600 A.D., he served as an Arab officer in the 630s in Syria, helping to seize the territory from the Byzantine Empire. In 640, Mu'awiyah become governor of the province, waging successful campaigns against the Byzantines to seize the islands of Cyprus and Rhodes. The death of the Caliph Uthman, however, brought Mu'awiyah in direct conflict with Muhammad's cousin, Ali ibn abi Talib, viewed by many as the legitimate caliph (and founder of the Shia sect). In 660, after defeating Ali, Mu'awiyah became caliph. He ruled until 680, and was an able administrator, but continued to be hated by the minority Shia.

Umar ibn al-Khatta. The second caliph, after Abu Bakr, ruling from 634 to 644 A.D. His rule corresponded with the first great expansion of the Muslims into Byzantine and Persian territories. In 636, Umar's armies took control of Damascus and Palestine from the Greeks and by 642 had seized Egypt from the Byzantines. The Arabs occupied the Persian capital of Ctesiphon in 638, and the strategic cities of Mosul and Babylon in 641.

Abd al-Malik ibn Marwan (646–705). was the Umayyad caliph from 685 to 705. After defeating rivals in Arabia and Iraq by the early 690s, Abd al-Malik began a period of reform and renewal to consolidate Islamic rule. He imposed Arabic as the official administrative language (replacing Greek and Persian), introduced new coins, reorganized the provinces of the empire, and began construction of the mosque in Jerusalem, the Dome of the Rock.

Muhammad bin Abdul Wahhab (1703–1792). He was a religious scholar and teacher, who founded the interpretation of Islam later known as Wahhabism. He had studied the Quran and other Islamic writings in Medina, Basra, and Damascus, and emerged from this instruction as a fierce fundamentalist, devoted to what he saw as the original intent of Allah in the Quran. He brought his learning and values back to the Nejd in 1742 and began to preach in support of an Islamic revival. In 1744, he formed an alliance with Muhammad bin Saud, emir and founder of the Saudi dynasty, to combine efforts, an alignment between politics and religion that continues to the present.

Muhammad bin Saud (r. 1744–1765). A tribal emir, he is considered the founder of the Saudi dynasty. From his domain in the town of Dariyah, in the central Nejd, he created a small state in alliance with the religious leader

Muhammad ibn 'Abd al-Wahhab at-Tamimi. Both believed that Islam had become corrupted, and campaigned for a stricter and more literal interpretation of the Quran and other Muslim religious teachings. Muhammad committed the Saud tribe to what would become known as the Wahhabi version of Islam, and set the pattern for future Saudi leaders.

Muhammad Ali Pasha, Egyptian ruler (1769–1849), of Balkan or Turkish origins, who established a strong state in Egypt, and occupied much of western Arabia. Encouraged by the Ottomans, he waged an ultimately unsuccessful attempt to conquer Arabia, 1811 to 1838. From his base in the Hijaz, he launched several expeditions against the Saudis and other tribes in the Nejd, but was unable to sustain his occupation, and withdrew his forces in the 1830s.

Faisal ibn Turki ibn Abdullah Al Saud (1785–1865). Saudi emir. After escaping from Egyptian captivity in 1838, he returned to the Nejd and declared himself emir. Gathering the old tribes and settlements together once again, he rallied his forces and retook Riyadh in 1843. He succeeded in retaking most of the original pre-1818 Saudi territory, excepting the Hijaz and the Hasa. Faisal strengthened the Saudi state and ruled until 1865, an uncharacteristically long reign in nineteenth-century Arabia. In 1850, however, a Saudi attempt to force tribute from Bahrain met the guns of the Royal Navy. Nonetheless, emir Faisal succeeded in consolidating control over central Arabia, resisting sporadic forays by sharifan forces. He died in 1865.

Turki ibn Abdullah ibn Muhammad, Saudi emir (1824–1834). Turki made Riyadh the new capital of the Saudi state. By the late 1820s, Turki had consolidated power in the Nejd, and turned east to the Hasa region along the Gulf Coast. Within a few years, he had gained authority over much of the region, exacting tribute from tribes along the coast. By 1830, the Saudis controlled most of the Hasa, but Turki's assassination in 1834 weakened this expansion.

Talil bin Abdullah al Rashid (r. 1847–1868). He was Rashidi tribal leader and created the Shammar tribal confederation. Under his role over central Arabia, allowed religious diversity within his territory, tolerating Shia Muslims, Jews, and Christians. Talil's eventual successor, Muhammad bin Rashid (1872–1897), began to expand from his base in Ha'il in the 1870s. Tribal affiliations and moderate policies ensured the initial success of the Rashidi state. Saudi fortunes were so low that even their capital, Riyadh, fell to the Rashidis in 1887, although a subsequent pro-Saudi uprising brought back the dynasty temporarily. In 1891, Rashid defeated the last army of the Saudis and occupied Riyadh.

Ibn Rashid (Mohammed bin Abdullah Al Rashid). One of the most prominent leaders of Al Rashid, an Arab tribe that was the chief rival to the Saudis in the Nejd for control over the peninsula in the mid-to-late nineteenth century. A client state of the Ottomans, the Rashidis were Sunni, but were more tolerant of outside influences and foreigners than the Saudis. The height of their rule came under Ibn Rashid, who from 1869 to 1897 ruled over almost all of what would later become central and eastern Saudi Arabia. Infighting over succession, and the weakening of their Ottoman sponsors, undermined the Rashidis and made them vulnerable to Saudi ascendancy in the early twentieth century.

Sharif Hussein bin Ali (1853–1931). He was the last emir of Mecca from the Hashemite family, who was most famous for leading the Arab Revolt against the Ottoman Empire during World War I. He was appointed by the Turks in 1908 as emir, and was a vassal of Istanbul, having lived in the Ottoman capital before receiving his position. Raised among Bedouins before being sent to Istanbul, he had strong tribal links to the Hijaz. In 1910, Hussein led an invasion of the western reaches of the Nejd, capturing Saad, Ibn Saud's brother. Although the sharifan army was too small to conquer the Hijaz, he was able to force Ibn Saud into a humiliating truce. Sharif Hussein ibn Ali, after being assured British support, declared an Arab Revolt in 1916, seized Mecca and declared himself King of the Arabs. After World War I, he ruled the Hijaz until 1924, when a Saudi offensive forced him into exile. He died in Jordan in 1931, but two of his sons became kings of Jordan and Iraq.

Abd al-Aziz ibn Al Saud (1876–1953). He became the first king of Saudi Arabia. Born in Riyadh, his family fled to exile in Kuwait in 1901. In 1901, Ibn Saud left Kuwait to raid the Rashidis in Arabia, and in 1902 retook Riyadh and declared himself emir. By 1912, he controlled much of the Nejd, and by 1922 defeated the Rashidis for control of the rest. In 1925, he conquered Mecca and the rest of the Hijaz, declaring himself king in January 1926. On September 23, 1932, Ibn Saud declared the creation of the Kingdom of Saudi Arabia, taking the title King Abd al-Aziz. He oversaw the discovery of oil in Saudi Arabia, and the beginnings of early modernization of the economy and state.

Faisal bin Hussein (1883–1933). The son of Sharif Hussein, Faisal led the Arab Revolt during World War I, alongside his British adviser T. E. Lawrence. After World War I, he briefly became King of Syria, but after being deposed in 1920 was installed by the United Kingdom as king of Iraq. He reigned until his death in 1933. His brother Abdullah became Transjordan's monarch.

T. (Thomas) E. (Edward) Lawrence (1888–1935). A graduate of Oxford, where he studied the architecture of the Middle East, Lawrence was an archaeologist who had worked in Syria, Lebanon, Egypt, and Iraq. After World War I began, he worked as a surveyor for the British government, and visited sites in Jordan and Arabia. He accepted a commission in the British Army in 1916, and was assigned to Cairo in 1916 because of his Arabic and his knowledge of the region. Also that year, he was sent to be adviser to Sharif Hussein of Mecca, who had launched a revolt against the Ottoman Empire. Accompanying the Arab rebels, Lawrence raided Turkish garrisons, helped take control of most of the Hijaz, and, most notably, seized the strategic port of Aqaba in 1917 and Damascus in October 1918. His hopes that the Arabs would become a united and independent state, under Sharif Hussein, did not come to fruition. The subject of significant media coverage, including several feature films, he became known worldwide as "Lawrence of Arabia."

Saud bin Abdul Aziz (1902–1969). He was crown prince during the 1930s, and became king after the death of King Abd al-Aziz in 1953. Although he created several essential ministries (water, education, and petroleum, among others), he was an ineffective monarch, who spent lavishly on himself and his favorites, squandering oil revenues. His palaces, massive entourage and harem, and other spending quickly created a national deficit and public humiliation, and in 1958 members of the royal family forced him to abdicate day-to-day power in favor of his more responsible brother, Faisal. In 1960, Saud temporarily regained the throne, but by 1962 Faisal had relegated him to a figurehead position. In 1964, Saud tried again to take power, but failed and went into permanent exile.

Faisal bin Abdul Aziz Al Saud (1906–1975). One of Ibn Saud's eldest sons, he held a variety of key positions under his father, including Minister of Foreign Affairs. He became crown prince when Saud became king in 1953. More competent and respected than his elder brother, in 1964 Faisal became king upon the forced abdication of Saud. Faisal restored the country's finances, presided over a long period of economic development, and became internationally respected as a leader in the Arab World, including through the 1973 oil boycott against nations that supported Israel. He was assassinated by a nephew in 1975.

Fahd bin Abdul Aziz Al Saud (1921–2005). King of Saudi Arabia. One of the elder sons of Ibn Saud, he served in a variety of positions under his father, including as Education Minister, Interior Minister, and envoy to the Arab League. He became Crown Prince under King Khalid in 1975, and exercised de facto control during the monarch's final years of failing health. He ruled Saudi Arabia during a time of domestic and international challenges, with falling oil prices, the Iranian Revolution, the Iran-Iraq War, and the Gulf War. In 1992 he introduced the Basic Law, and began other reform, but suffered a debilitating stroke in 1995, and day-to-day governance passed to his crown prince, Abdullah.

Abdullah Abdullah bin Abdul Aziz Al Saud (1924–present). King of Saudi Arabia (2005–present). He was crown prince under King Fahd, and became regent and acting ruler upon the king's stroke in 1995. Considered progressive in the context of Saudi Arabia's strict Islam, he has encouraged modest reforms, such as municipal elections and the creation of the Allegiance Council to name future monarchs.

Glossary

Abaya—The traditional clothing worn by Muslim women in much of the Arabian peninsula, it is an overgarment designed to cover the entire body, other than the head and hands. Typically black, it is mandatory for women in Saudi Arabia, and is often accompanied by a face veil.

Abbasid—An Arab Islamic dynasty that ruled from 750 to 1258 A.D., it ruled over a vast Sunni population, from Spain to Persia. The Abbasids moved their capital from Damascus to Baghdad, where they reigned until being overrun by the Mongols.

Allah—Arabic word for "God," it is also used by non-Arabic-speaking Muslims, and Arabic-speaking Christians and Jews.

Arab—ethnic, political and/or linguistic group that predominates in the Middle East. Tracing their origins to the Arabian Peninsula, there are 200–350 million Arabs, depending on the definition of the term.

Arab League—an international organization of 22 Arab states, founded in 1945 to promote unity in the Middle East and North Africa, to oppose the creation of Israel, and to limit external influence in the region.

Saudi Aramco—Formerly known as Aramco (Arab-American Oil Company), this is the official state-run oil corporation of Saudi Arabia, which controls extraction, refining, and exporting of all oil and natural gas. Formed in the 1930s as a private corporation, it gradually became state-owned in the 1970s, until 1980 when this process was complete. It controls 25 percent of the world's known reserves of petroleum.

Ashura—Shia festival commemorating the martyrdom in 680 A.D. of Hussein bin Ali, grandson of Muhammad. Along with his father, Ali, Hussein is considered one of the holy imams and founder of Shia Islam.

Bedouin—Traditional desert Arab nomads, who until the twentieth century survived through raiding, commerce, and animal husbandry. Few genuine nomads live in Saudi Arabia, but the customs and culture of the Bedouin remain strong.

Caliph—head of state or leader of Muslims, also known as the successors to the Prophet Muhammad. During the centuries of Islamic ascendancy, Arab caliphs ruled over the Middle East and beyond. Beginning in the sixteenth century, Ottoman Turkish rulers claimed the title, and held it until it was abolished in 1924.

Emir—title for tribal chieftain or other local or regional leader.

Fatimids—A Shia dynasty, within the Ismaili branch, that ruled Egypt and much of North Africa and the Levant from 910 to 1171.

Fatwa—a religious decree issued by a Muslim scholar or scholars, interpreting Islamic law to provide guidance on a major issue or question. Examples could include declaring a government legitimate, endorsing a war, or prohibiting certain behaviors.

Five Pillars of Islam—These are the fundamentals practices of the faith, and are: prayer (five times daily, facing Mecca), making the pilgrimage to Mecca, paying alms, fasting during the month of Ramadan, and professing the faith.

Gulf Cooperation Council—An international organization of conservative monarchies in the Persian Gulf area. The GCC formed in 1981, and is led by Saudi Arabia. Its purposes are to promote common defense, promote regional cooperation, and coordinate cultural, scientific, and technological ventures. Its membership consists of Saudia Arabia, Kuwait, Bahrain, Qatar, the United Arab Emirates, Oman.

Hadith—These are collections of the non-Quranic writings and sayings of the Prophet Muhammad. There is significant dispute between scholars and religious leaders within the Islamic world, especially between Shia and Sunni, about the provenance and applicability of the thousands of these writings still extant.

Hajj—The pilgrimage to Mecca, one of the pillars of Islam. Every Muslim who is able should make this trip at least once. The poor and physically unable are exempt from this requirement. One who completes the pilgrimage is known as a hajji, a title of respect in the Islamic world.

Hanbalism—One of the four most important schools of Sunni Islamic law, and the most conservative. Its founder, Ahmad bin Hanbal, taught a literal interpretation of the Quran and other Islamic texts. Emerging in the ninth century, it is the antecedent of more recent fundamentalist schools of Islam, including Wahhabism.

Hasa—the eastern zone of the Arabian Peninsula, within modern Saudi Arabia. It holds the vast majority of oil reserves, and also the largest numbers of Shia Muslims within the kingdom.

Hashemites—An Arab dynasty in the Hijaz of western Arabia, descended from Muhammad. They were the traditional rulers over Mecca and Medina, both as independent monarchs and as clients of the Ottomans, until the twentieth century. After the Saudi conquest of the Hijaz in 1925, Hashemite kings ruled Syria (1920), Iraq (1921–1958), and Jordan (1921–present).

Hijaz—the western coastal zone of Arabia, including Mecca, Medina, and Jeddah. Historically the most developed area of the peninsula, it hosts the annual Muslim pilgrimage.

Ikhwan—Arab military order under the Saudi dynasty, it was an essential part of the Saudi system. Comprised of fervent followers of Wahhabi Islam, it was the shock force of the Saudis until the 1920s, when it rebelled against King Ibn Saud. The monarch defeated and repressed the Ikhwan in 1929, although some members were allowed to join the new Saudi National Guard.

Imam—an Islamic religious leader, teacher, or other important figure within the faith

Islam—faith promulgated by the Prophet Muhammad, it literally means "submission," as a followed is expected to submit to Allah.

Jihad—a holy war in Islam, which can be an internal struggle within a believer's soul, or an external battle against enemies of the faith.

Ka'bah—"cube"—This structure stands in Mecca, and is the center of the pilgrimage. Made of brick and masonry, it serves as the symbolic center, around which pilgrims walk seven times to show their devotion to God.

Kharijite—a dissident branch of Shia Islam, emerging in the seventh century A.D., that promoted egalitarianism, ongoing jihad, and strict fundamentalism. In 661, they killed Ali, founder of Shia Islam, and also remained enemies of the mainstream Sunni caliphate. Although embraced by peripheral groups in the Middle East and North Africa, they remained a distinct minority, known mostly because of their role in the death of Ali.

Majlis—daily or weekly audiences held by the kings of Saudi Arabia, to hear petitions from subjects, decide on matters of state, and adjudicate disputes.

Mosque—Muslim place of worship

Mujahideen—holy warriors in Islam, this word can refer to any Muslim fighting a religious war or battle, whether against Muslims or non-Muslims. During the 1980s, it most often referred to the Saudi-supported rebels fighting against the Soviet Union in Afghanistan.

Muslim—follower of Islam; "one who submits."

Nejd—central region of the Arabian Peninsula; mostly desert. It was the area that saw the origin of the Saudi dynasty, as well as the Wahhabi tendency within Islam.

OPEC—Organization of Petroleum Exporting Countries. Founded in 1960, OPEC's goals are to control global oil prices, continue to ensure the predictable flow of petroleum, and coordinate production levels. Its members are mostly, but not all, Middle Eastern nations such as Saudi Arabia, Kuwait, Iran, and Iraq. Saudi Arabia is the largest oil producer within OPEC and the world.

Quran—The holy book of Islam, as delivered to the Prophet Muhammad by the Angel Gabriel in the early seventh century. It consists of 114 chapters in Arabic. Originally conveyed orally by Muhammad to his followers for their memorization, it was written down in the mid-seventh century.

Sharia—Islamic law and tradition, based on the Quran and Hadith, and interpreted through the five major schools of law. Sharia includes family law, criminal law, and civil law, and other areas of jurisprudence, and is understood to be all-encompassing as a legal system.

Sheikh—Arab tribal leader.

Shi'ite—Minority denomination within Islam, comprising approximately 15 percent of Muslims worldwide. Shia trace their origins to Ali, the son-in-law of Muhammad, and Ali's son, Hussein. They follow the Five Pillars of Islam, but revere Ali and Hussein and regard the Sunni caliphs after Muhammad as illegitimate. See Ali.

Sunni—majority denomination within Islam, representing approximately 80 percent of Muslims worldwide. They follow the Five Pillars of Islam, and regard the Sunni caliphates, and the legal and religious legacy that followed, as legitimate.

Ulama—a group of religious scholars

Umayyad—A Sunni Arab dynasty, it ruled over the first caliphate from 661 to 750 A.D. The Umayyads expanded the Islam faith to its greatest extent during this period.

Ummah—"community" in Arabic, it most often refers to the community of all believers in Islam.

Annotated Bibliography

Despite its importance over the past few decades, the history of Arabia, especially those regions that in the twentieth century would become Saudi Arabia, is less documented and researched than almost any major country in history, especially in the West. Among the most important factors contributing to this dearth of sources are the centuries of a mostly oral culture, the absence of a large population base, and the dispersal of Arabs from the peninsula to other territories during and after the period of Islamic expansion. In modern times, the Saudi state has also been an obstacle, not only because of its indifference until recently toward archaeological and historical work on pre-Islamic civilizations, but because of its restrictions on intellectual freedom, archival access, and research by foreigners.

Saudi universities, none of which predate the mid-twentieth century, have emphasized subjects such as engineering, science, and Islamic studies, rather than humanities or social sciences, and so have trained few historians or specialists in similar fields. Tourism, which has encouraged historical work in neighboring nations such as Jordan and Saudi, is minimal in Saudi Arabia. The Saudi government, again unlike other regional governments, has not funded international research about its history or heritage, other than through narrow support to sympathetic Islamic scholars. As such, the sum of serious works on the history of Saudi Arabia is less substantial than would otherwise be expected, and is focused almost exclusively on the modern period. Until recent decades, it was just possible for a scholar of Saudi Arabia to read almost every book of significance in the field, at least those published in English and Arabic.

This bibliography includes the most accessible books published in English since 1950, but excludes academic journals, magazines, and other periodicals, both professional and popular. There is also a significant number of Web sites that present information about Saudi Arabia, but the ephemeral nature and uncertain reliability of the Internet should stand as a caution against the use of its sites for historical research, beyond acquiring a general familiarity with the subject.

Saudi Arabia is a relatively new state, only taking its final form in the 1920s, with its name and political system becoming official in 1932. Because of its history before the twentieth century is hard to understand as distinct. Many of the major historical actors or developments were not confined to the modern borders of Saudi Arabia. As such, the terms *Arabia* and *Arabian Peninsula* figure larger in early works in the field, accurate for their periods but without the precision of the mostly defined boundaries of later Saudi Arabia.

General Works

There are several excellent works that examine the entire history of the territory that in the twentieth century became Saudi Arabia. The most accessible text is James Wynbrandt, *A Brief History of Saudi Arabia* (New York: Facts on File, 2004), which includes events from prehistory to Operation Iraqi Freedom. The definitive scholarly treatment is Madawi al-Rasheed, *A History of Saudi Arabia* (Cambridge: Cambridge University Press, 2002), while a more dense version is Alexei Vassiliev, *The History of Saudi Arabia* (London: Saqi, 2000). Both of these texts begin with the rise of the Saudi dynasty in central Arabia. An invaluable resource is the annotated bibliography, Frank Clements, *Saudi Arabia* (World Bibliographical Series) (Oxford, UK: ABC-Clio Press, 1988).

Saudi Arabia also receives significant mention in more general works about the Arabs and Islam, including the readable Albert Hourani, *A History of the Arab Peoples* (New York: Warner Books, 1991); slightly dated, but still encyclopedic are Philip Hitti, *History of the Arabs,* 10th edition (New York: St. Martin's Press, 1970) and Bernard Lewis, *The Arabs in History* (London: Hutchinson, 1954); a broader account of Muslim communities through history is John Esposito, ed., *The Oxford History of Islam* (Oxford, UK: Oxford University Press, 1999), which includes useful chapters on the origin and spread of Arab Islam. An interesting sociological study is Joel Carmichael, *The Shaping of the Arabs: A Study of Ethnic Identity* (New York: Macmillan, 1967), although its conclusions are sometimes questionable.

Arabia before Muhammad (to 570 A.D.)

The history of ancient Arabia is primarily peripheral; the most significant developments occurred not because the Arabs were central to civilization, but because they were on the periphery of those states that were. The most important Arab or semi-Arab civilization was that of the Nabataeans, which flourished along the northern reaches of the peninsula, most famously in the ancient city of Petra, in modern-day Jordan. Among the works that examine this civilization, tied as it was to the ancient empires of the Greeks and Romans, are Avraham Negev, *Nabataean Archaeology Today* (New York: New York University Press, 1986); Joseph Patrich, *The Formation of Nabataean Art* (Jerusalem: Hebrew University, 1990); John Healey, *The Nabataean Tomb Inscriptions of Mada'in Salih* (Oxford: Oxford University Press, 1993); and Jane Taylor, *Petra and the Lost Kingdoms of the Nabataeans* (Cambridge, MA: Harvard University Press, 2002).

Rome's impact on the Arabs came primarily through its wars involving the Nabataeans, as well as its occupation of the kingdom in 106 A.D. Several emperors, including Septimus Severus and Philip, had close ties to the region. The most well-researched and substantial study of the Roman impact on Arabia is G. W. Bowersock, *Roman Arabia* (Cambridge, MA: Harvard University Press, 1983). Another study uses archaeological, climatic, and other data to examine the population and other changes brought by Roman conquest: Henry Innes MacAdam, *Geography, Urbanisation and Settlement Patterns in the Roman Near East* (Aldershot, Hampshire, UK: Ashgate, 2002). The imperial army that repressed the Jews, fought rebellious Arabs, and brought order to the region receives thorough treatment in D. L. Kennedy, *The Roman Army in Jordan* (London: British Academy, 2000).

Other useful works relevant to ancient Arabia, especially on its geographic periphery, include David Graf, *Rome and the Arabian Frontiers from the Nabataeans to the Saracens* (Aldershot, Hampshire, UK: Ashgate, 1997); Gordon Newby, *A History of the Jews of Arabia* (Columbia: University of South Carolina Press, 1988); Paul Johnson, Civilizations of the Holy Land (London: Weidenfeld and Nicolson, 1990); D. T. Potts, *The Arabian Gulf in Antiquity,* vols. 1 and 2 (Oxford, UK: Oxford University Press, 1990); and Klaus Schippmann, *Ancient South Arabia: From the Queen of Sheba to the Advent of Islam* (Princeton, NJ: Markus Wiener, 2002).

Arabia from Muhammad to the Saudis

The rise of Islam in the Arabian Peninsula, and its broader impact on the world, is arguably the most important event in the history of the Arab people. As such, the life and religious activity of the Prophet Muhammad has received significant attention. Among the accessible biographies of Muhammad are the short volume by Michael Cook, *Muhammad* (Oxford, UK: Oxford University Press, 1996) and the more thorough text by Karen Armstrong, *Muhammad: A Prophet for Our Times* (London: Eminent Books, 2006). The cities of Mecca and Medina, the two locations that witnessed the early years of the faith, and became centers for Muslim pilgrimage, are examined in Philip Hitti, *Capital Cities of Arab Islam* (Minneapolis: University of Minnesota Press, 1973); F. E. Peters, *Mecca: A Literary History of the Muslim Holy Land* (Princeton: Princeton University Press, 1994); and Gerald de Gaury, *Rulers of Mecca* (London: George G. Garrap, 1951).

The hajj, the pilgrimage to Mecca, has drawn interest, particularly in its impact on the Hijaz, detailed in John Burckhardt, *Travels in Arabia* (Charleston, SC: Biblio Bazaar, 2006—reprint from 1829); Suraiya Faroqhi, *Pilgrims and Sultans: The Hajj under the Ottomans, 1517–1683* (New York: I. B. Tauris, 1994); and William Oschenwald, *Religion, Society and the State in Arabia: The Hijaz under Ottoman Control, 1840–1908* (Columbus: Ohio State University Press, 1984). The history of the region from Muhammad to the rise of the Saud dynasty also receives attention in the biographical sketch by Philip K. Hitti, *Makers of Arab History* (New York: Harper, 1968); the military and political account of Amin Maalouf, *The Crusades Through Arab Eyes* (New York: Schocken/Random House, 1984); and Linda George, *The Golden Age of Islam* (New York: Benchmark, 1998). Also useful as a clear account of the first 500 years of conflict within Islam, especially between Sunni and Shia, is F. E. Peters, *Allah's Commonwealth: A History of Islam in the Near East, 600–1100 A.D.* (New York: Simon and Schuster, 1973).

Saudi Arabia

If previous centuries are characterized by a dearth of solid historical work on the Arabian Peninsula, at least in comparison to other regions, the last century has produced scores of texts. The remarkable rise of the Saudi state, in the midst of Ottoman decline, Western imperialism, and threats posed by internal rivals, captivated many Westerners. While other Westerners published memoirs of their sojourns in the peninsula, none continue to hold as much interest as that by Lawrence of Arabia: T. E. Lawrence, *Seven Pillars of Wisdom* (Garden City, NY: Doubleday, 1935), who recounts his desert adventures during the Arab Revolt of World War I, as well as the collapse of his hopes for a united Arab nation.

The origins of the Saudi dynasty have received some attention, but the historical record has left limited sources in this regard. Two helpful works that provide the more general context for this emergence are J. M. Wagstaff, *The Evolution of Middle Eastern Landscapes: An Outline to A.D. 1840* (London: Croom

Helm, 1985), and Charles Didier, *Sojourn with the Grand Sharif of Makkah* (New York: Oleander, 1985).

The singular figure of Abd al Aziz, or Ibn Saud, the first and most important king of Saudi Arabia, has been the focus of many works. While earlier accounts such as Ahmed Assah, *Miracle of the Desert Kingdom* (London: Johnson, 1969), H. St. John Philby, *Saudi Arabia* (New York: Frederick A. Praeger, 1955), and David Howart, *The Desert King: Ibn Saud and His Arabia* (New York: McGraw Hill, 1964) tend toward hagiography, more recent scholarship presents a more balanced perspective, including David Holden and Richard Johns, *The House of Saud* (New York: Holt, Rinehart and Winston, 1981); Robert Lacey, *The Kingdom: Arabia and the House of Saud* (New York: Harcourt, Brace and Jovanovich, 1982); and Alexander Bligh, *From Prince to King: Royal Succession in the House of Saud in the 20th Century* (New York: New York University Press, 1984).

In the midst of greater attention to the first Saudi monarch, broader historical developments that led to the creation of independent states in the aftermath of the Ottoman collapse are the focus of Frederick Anscombe, *The Ottoman Gulf: The Creation of Kuwait, Saudi Arabia and Qatar* (New York: Columbia University Press, 1997) and Ian Richard Netton, ed., *Arabia and the Gulf: From Traditional Society to Modern States* (London: Croom Helm, 1986).

The relationship between Saudi Arabia and the United States, as well as the reaction of Saudi Arabia to Islamic terrorism, has drawn the attention of other authors. Among these are the somewhat exaggerated Stephen Schwartz, *The Two Faces of Islam: The House of Sa'ud from Tradition to Terror* (New York: Doubleday, 2002), and the more measured Thomas Lippman, *Inside the Mirage: America's Fragile Partnership with Saudi Arabia* (Boulder, CO: Westview, 2004). Ideological currents in the twentieth-century Arab world, including nationalism, Arab socialism, and Baathism, receive attention in Zeine Zeine, *The Emergence of Arab Nationalism* (Beirut, Lebanon: Khayats, 1966).

More recent works on Saudi Arabia and modern Islam have taken a more sociological or journalistic approach, and include Reza Aslan, *No God But God: The Origins, Evolution, and Future of Islam* (New York: Random House, 2006); Sandra Mackey, *The Saudis: Inside the Desert Kingdom* (New York: W. W. Norton, 2002); and Geoff Simons, *Saudi Arabia: The Shape of Client Feudalism* (New York: St. Martin's Press, 1998).

Index

About the Author

WAYNE H. BOWEN is Associate Professor of History at Ouachita Baptist University, Arkansas.

Other Titles in the Greenwood Histories of the Modern Nations
Frank W. Thackeray and John E. Findling, Series Editors

The History of Argentina
Daniel K. Lewis

The History of Australia
Frank G. Clarke

The History of the Baltic States
Kevin O'Connor

The History of Brazil
Robert M. Levine

The History of Canada
Scott W. See

The History of Central America
Thomas Pearcy

The History of Chile
John L. Rector

The History of China
David C. Wright

The History of Congo
Didier Gondola

The History of Cuba
Clifford L. Staten

The History of Egypt
Glenn E. Perry

The History of Ethiopia
Saheed Adejumobi

The History of Finland
Jason Lavery

The History of France
W. Scott Haine

The History of Germany
Eleanor L. Turk

The History of Ghana
Roger S. Gocking

The History of Great Britain
Anne Baltz Rodrick

The History of Holland
Mark T. Hooker

The History of India
John McLeod

The History of Indonesia
Steven Drakeley

The History of Iran
Elton L. Daniel

The History of Iraq
Courtney Hunt

The History of Ireland
Daniel Webster Hollis III

The History of Israel
Arnold Blumberg

The History of Italy
Charles L. Killinger

The History of Japan
Louis G. Perez

The History of Korea
Djun Kil Kim

The History of Kuwait
Michael S. Casey

The History of Mexico
Burton Kirkwood

The History of New Zealand
Tom Brooking